AQA
GCSE PHYSICS
ADDITIONS

Steve Witney

Hodder & Stoughton
A MEMBER OF THE HODDER HEADLINE GROUP

Contents

About this book iii

Specification Matching Grids iv

Ideas and evidence in Science iv

Chapter 1 1

Chapter 2 22

Chapter 3 45

Glossary 54

Index 55

About this book

The contents

The contents of this book are designed to cover all aspects of the knowledge and understanding required by the AQA GCSE specifications in Physics (Co-ordinated) and Physics (Modular).

The subject content required by the KS4 Double Award specification for Physical processes attainment target is produced in a format identical to that used in the Hodder and Stoughton textbook *AQA GCSE Science*. This core material is supplemented by the additional subject content required for the specification in GCSE Physics.

What is in each chapter?

At the beginning of each chapter is a list of **Key Terms**. Where used for the first time, these key terms are emboldened. Some of the key terms are coloured. These are the extra terms you will need to know if you are going to be entered for the Higher tier papers in the final examination. All the key terms together with their meanings are also found in the **Glossary** on page 54.

The contents of each chapter are divided into several sections. Each section concentrates on one topic. A symbol at the start of each section shows clearly which topic from the co-ordinated and modular courses is being targeted.

You will see a number of **Did you know?** boxes throughout each chapter. You will not have to learn the information in these boxes, but they are there to give extra interest to the topic.

At the end of various sections, you will find a number of **Topic Questions**. Because the topic questions have been designd to produce answers that you could use as a set of revision notes, it is recommended that you write down the questions as well as the answers. The questions written on a yellow background are the more demanding questions, expected to be answered if you are a grade B/A/A★ student. Don't worry if you have to re-read the topic again when you try to answer these questions. This will help you to learn the work.

At the end of each chapter is a **Summary**. The summary provides a brief analysis of the important points covered in the section.

Completing each chapter are some **GCSE questions** taken from past AQA (SEG) or past AQA (NEAB) examination papers. The questions written on a yellow background are the more demanding questions expected to be answered if you are a grade B/A/A★ student. Answering the GCSE questions will help give you an idea of what is wanted when you take your final science examination. Again, do not worry if you have to go back to read the work again. The examination questions may well test you on knowledge not included in the particular chapter. Don't worry – look through the other chapters to find the extra information you need to complete our answer.

Specification Matching Grids

Specification Matching Grid

Content				AQA specification references	
				Co-ordinated	Modular
Chapter		Section			
1 Electricity		1.1	Control in circuits	10.6	23 (14.1 – 14.6)
2 Forces and Motion		2.1	Turning forces	10.10	24 (15.1 – 15.2)
		2.2	Momentum	10.11	24 (15.4)
		2.3	Circular motion	10.12	24 (15.3)
3 Waves		3.1	Optical devices	10.15	23 (14.7)

Ideas and evidence in Science

Section	DA	Core/HT	Context
1.1	✓	core	Advantages and disadvantages of advanced electronic systems

Chapter 1
Electricity

Key terms: capacitor • input sensor • logic gate • output device • potential divider • processor • relay • resistor • transistor

1.1 Control in circuits

Co-ordinated	Modular
10.6	14.1 to 14.6 mod 23

Switches

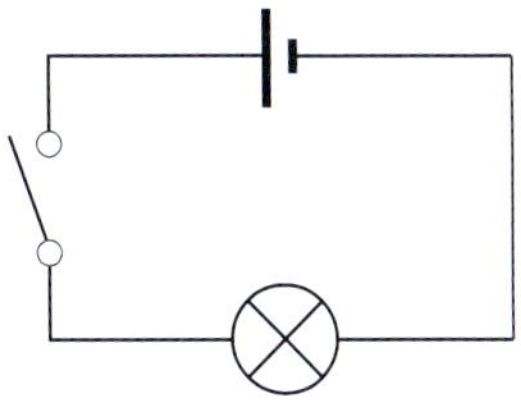

A switch is one way to control a device in a circuit. In Figure 1.1 a simple switch is used to control a lamp.

Closing the switch (the switch is ON) completes the circuit. A current will flow through the switch and the lamp will light.

Opening the switch (the switch is OFF) creates a break in the circuit. A current cannot flow through the switch so the lamp is off.

Not all switches are this simple. A **transistor** can be used as a high speed electronic switch (see pages 13–15).

Figure 1.1

Relays

Figure 1.2
Relay switches

A **relay** is a switch worked by an electromagnet. A small current in the input circuit can be used to switch on a larger current in the separate output circuit. This makes the relay a useful switch to use in an electronic circuit (see page 10).

Electricity

Figure 1.3

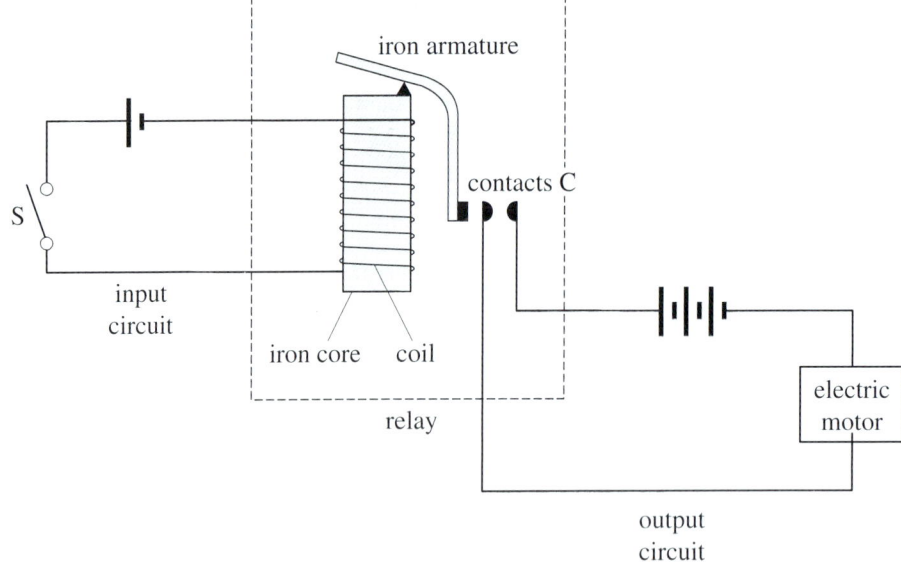

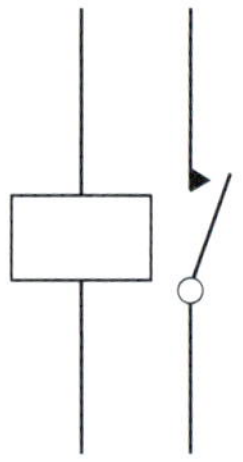

Figure 1.4 ▲
A circuit symbol for a normally open relay

Figure 1.3 shows how a relay can be used to switch on an electric motor. Closing the switch S completes the input circuit. A small current then flows through the coil, magnetizing the iron core. This attracts the iron armature, which as it pivots closes the contacts C. The output circuit is now complete and a current flows through the motor. This type of relay is called a 'normally open' relay. When the input switch is OFF (open), the contacts C are open, so the output circuit is OFF.

Robotic machines are usually computer controlled. The small current from the computer operates relays that switch on the larger currents needed to operate and control the robot.

Figure 1.5 ▶
A robot used to build cars

Did you know?
In 1920 the Czech, Karel Copek, wrote a play about slave-like machines. The Czech word for this is *Robota*.

Resistors

The current through a circuit can be controlled using a fixed **resistor** or a variable resistor.

The fixed resistors used in electronic circuits often have coloured bands painted around them.

Control in Circuits

Figure 1.6
A circuit board containing resistors

The colours are part of a code used to indicate the value of the resistor and the tolerance (or accuracy) to which it is made.

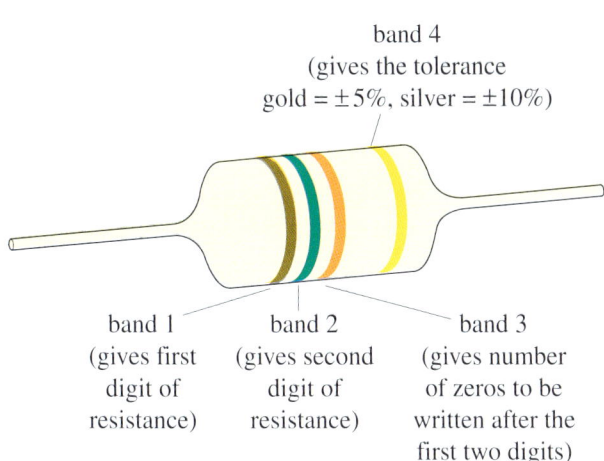

Colour	Figure
Black	0
Brown	1
Red	2
Orange	3
Yellow	4
Green	5
Blue	6
Violet	7
Grey	8
White	9

Figure 1.7
A resistor

band 4
(gives the tolerance
gold = ±5%, silver = ±10%)

band 1 (gives first digit of resistance)
band 2 (gives second digit of resistance)
band 3 (gives number of zeros to be written after the first two digits)

Figure 1.8
The resistor colour code

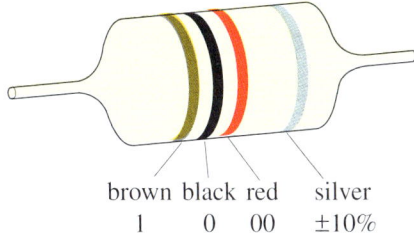

brown black red   silver
  1   0   00   ±10%

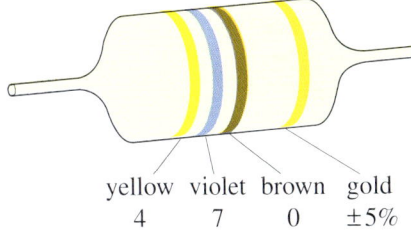

yellow violet brown gold
  4   7   0   ±5%

Figure 1.9
Resistance = 1000 ohms ± 10%
(note: 1000 ohms = 1 kilohm)

Figure 1.10
Resistance = 470 ohms ± 5%

A variable resistor can be used to vary the current in a circuit. The resistor consists of a long length of wire and a sliding contact. Moving the contact changes the resistance by changing the length of wire in the circuit.

Electricity

Figure 1.11
A variable resistor

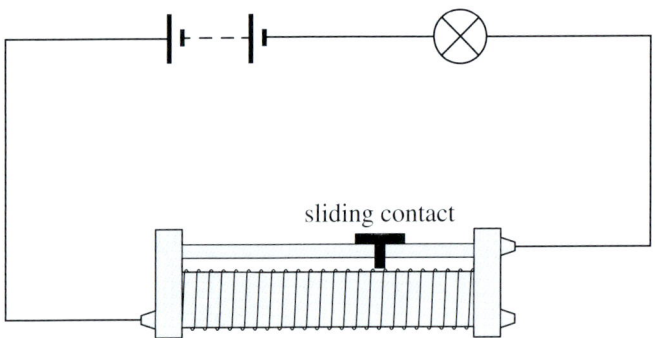

Moving the sliding contact to the left reduces the length of wire in the circuit. This reduces the resistance and increases the current. So the bulb gets brighter.

In radios, small variable resistors are used as volume controls. Turning the centre spindle changes the resistance and so changes the volume.

Figure 1.12
The volume control on a radio is a variable resistor

Topic questions

1. The diagram shows a simple circuit.

   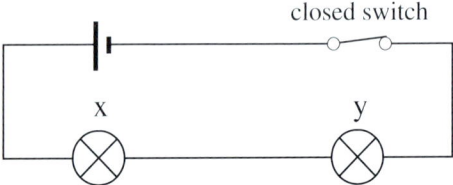

   What will happen to each lamp when the switch is opened? Give a reason for your answer.

2. The lamps in the circuit are identical.

   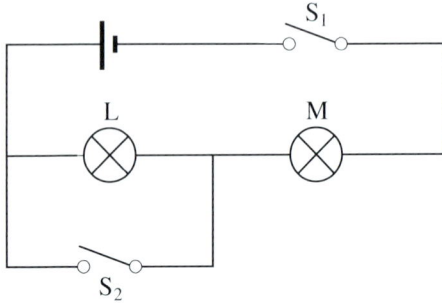

   Explain what happens to each lamp when:
   a) only switch S1 is closed;
   b) only switch S2 is closed;
   c) switch S1 and switch S2 are closed.

4

Control in Circuits

3 The diagram shows the position of the relay contacts when no current flows through the electromagnet.

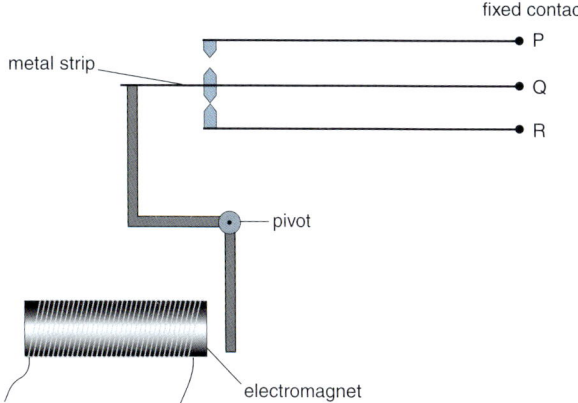

a) Which of the contacts are joined together?

A current is then passed through the electromagnet.
b) In which direction does the metal strip move?
c) Which contacts are now joined together?

4 The circuit diagram shows a relay used to turn on an electric motor. Explain, step by step, why the motor turns on when switch S is closed.

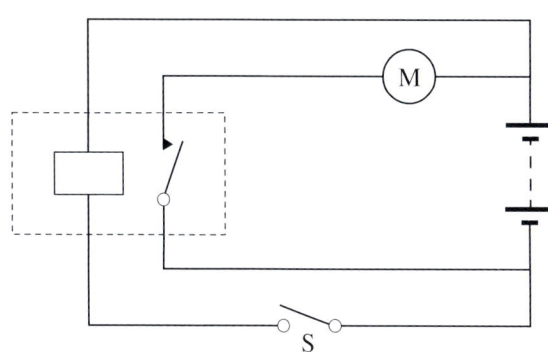

5 The diagram shows four resistors K, L, M and N. What is the value of each resistor?

K
brown, red, brown, silver

L
blue, grey, red, silver

M
orange, white, black, gold

N
green, brown, orange, gold

6 What are the colours of the first three bands of the following value resistors?
   a) 150 ohms
   b) 11 ohms
   c) 43 kilohms
   d) 9.1 kilohms

7 A resistor has the following colour code:

orange   orange   orange   silver

What are the maximum and minimum values this resistor can have?

Electricity

Electronic systems

Many electronic systems are designed in three parts, the **input sensors**, the **processor** and the **output device**. Systems can be shown as block diagrams. The arrows show the direction in which the signal or information is passed.

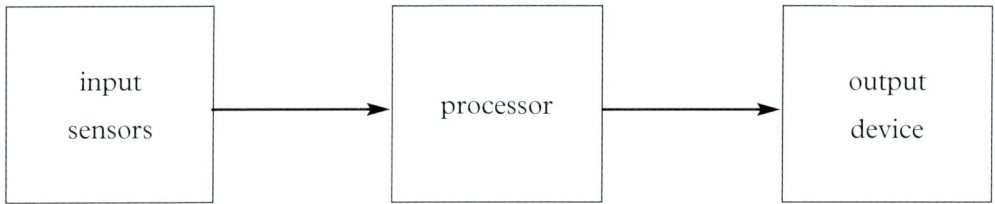

Input sensors detect changes in the environment. A sensor produces an electrical signal by transferring energy from one form (e.g. light) into electrical energy.

Input sensors include:

- Thermistors which detect changes in temperature.
- LDRs (light dependent resistors), which detect changes in light intensity.
- Microphones which respond to changes in sound intensity.
- Switches which respond to pressure, tilt, magnetic fields or moisture.

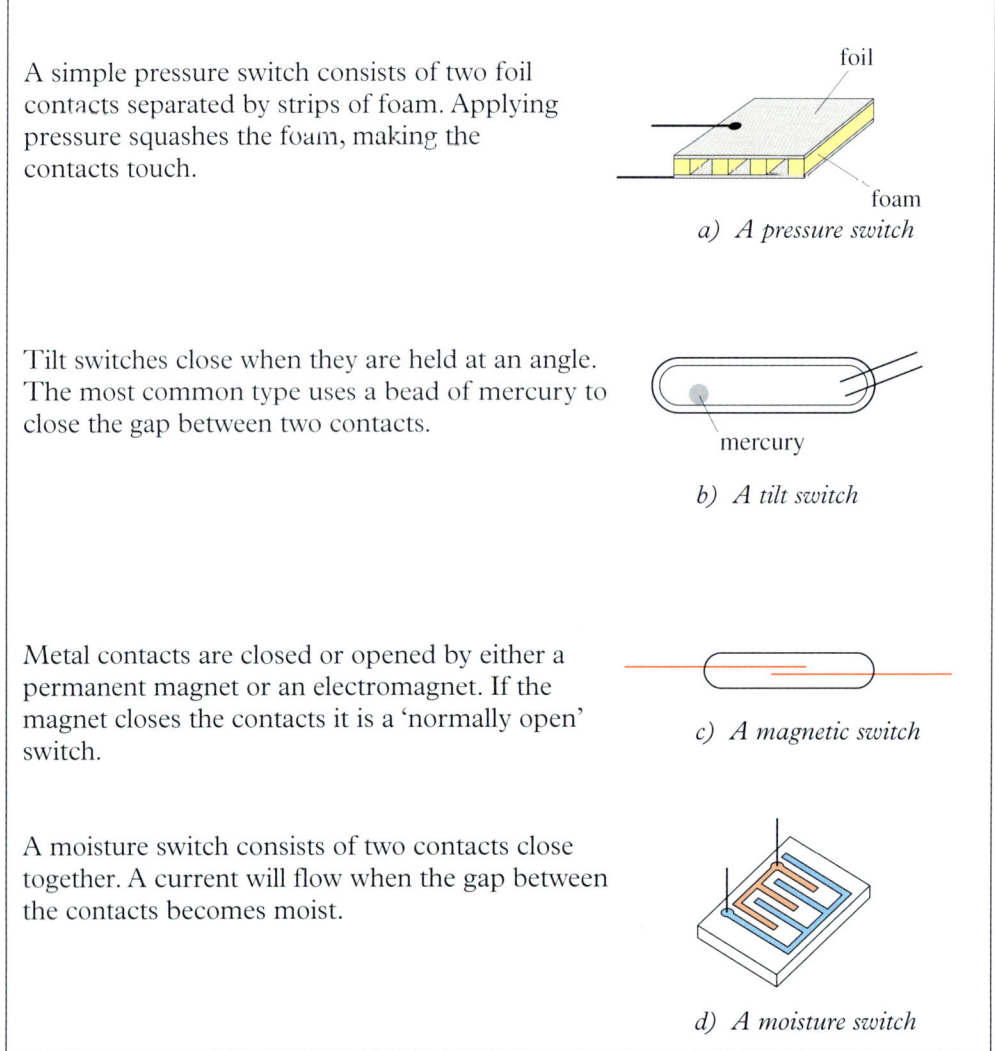

A simple pressure switch consists of two foil contacts separated by strips of foam. Applying pressure squashes the foam, making the contacts touch.

a) *A pressure switch*

Tilt switches close when they are held at an angle. The most common type uses a bead of mercury to close the gap between two contacts.

b) *A tilt switch*

Metal contacts are closed or opened by either a permanent magnet or an electromagnet. If the magnet closes the contacts it is a 'normally open' switch.

c) *A magnetic switch*

A moisture switch consists of two contacts close together. A current will flow when the gap between the contacts becomes moist.

d) *A moisture switch*

Figure 1.13 *Types of input sensor*

Control in Circuits

> **Did you know?**
>
>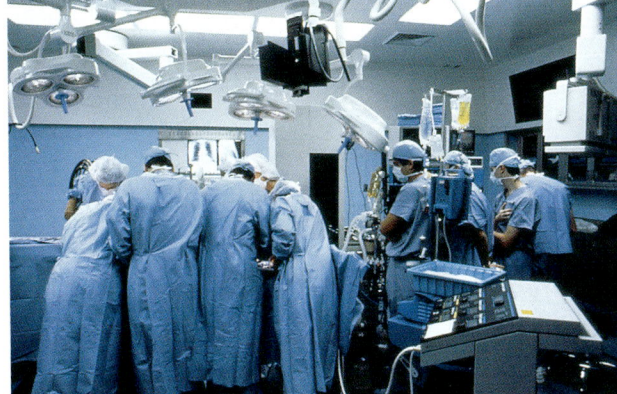
>
> **Figure 1.14**
>
> A hospital anaesthetist can use an infrared sensor to measure the carbon dioxide concentration in the air breathed out by a patient.

A processor takes the information from the input sensors and decides what action is needed. Processors can be made using logic gates (see page 9).

The output device is controlled by the processor. It transfers electrical energy supplied by the processor into other forms of energy.

Output devices include:

Figure 1.15
An LED

- Lamps which produce light.
- LEDs which produce light.
- Buzzers which produce sound.
- Electric motors which produce movement.
- Electric heaters which produce heat.
- Loudspeakers which produce sound.

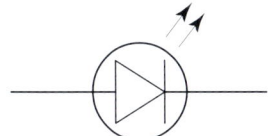

Figure 1.16
LED circuit symbol

An LED (light emitting diode) is a special type of diode that glows when a small current passes through it. LEDs are often used as indicator lamps (on/off).

Logic Gates

Logic gates are switches used to control a wide range of devices. They are called gates because they only 'open' to produce an output signal for the right combination of input signals.

The circuits shown in Figures 1.17 and 1.19 are simple examples of logic gates. In each circuit the output from the lamp is determined by the inputs from the switches.

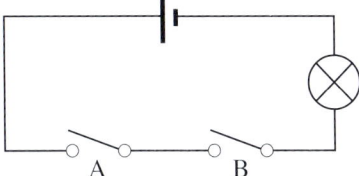

Figure 1.17
AND logic gate

Switch A	Switch B	Lamp output
open	open	OFF
open	closed	OFF
closed	open	OFF
closed	closed	ON

Figure 1.18
AND gate truth table

The lamp is ON when switch A AND switch B are closed.

Electricity

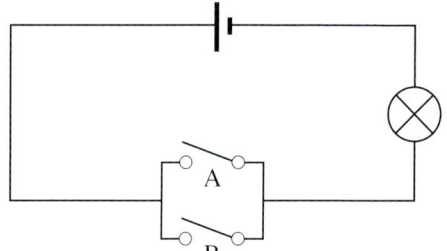

Switch A	Switch B	Lamp output
open	open	OFF
open	closed	ON
closed	open	ON
closed	closed	ON

Figure 1.20
OR gate truth table

Figure 1.19
OR logic gate

Did you know?
The invention of the transistor in 1947 was the first step towards miniature electronic circuits. The transistor replaced the much larger thermionic valve.

The lamp is ON when switch A OR switch B OR both switches are closed.

Figures 1.18 and 1.20 show the output from the lamp for every possible switch position. This sort of table is called a truth table.

In practice logic gates are made using combinations of transistors as the switches. This means they can be switched on and off millions of times a second.

AND, OR and NOT gates

In any circuit the inputs to a logic gate and the output from a logic gate can only be ON or OFF. An input or output that is ON is said to be HIGH. This is called logic state '1'. An input or output that is OFF is said to be LOW. This is called logic state '0'.

The three basic types of logic gate are called AND, OR and NOT. The circuit symbol and truth table for each of these gates is given in Figure 1.21.

AND

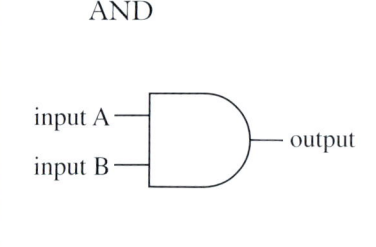

Input A	Input B	Output
0	0	0
0	1	0
1	0	0
1	1	1

This has two inputs and one output. For the output to be ON (1), input A AND input B must both be ON (1).

OR

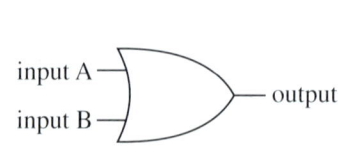

Input A	Input B	Output
0	0	0
0	1	1
1	0	1
1	1	1

This has two inputs and one output. For the output to be ON (1), input A OR input B OR both, must be ON (1).

NOT

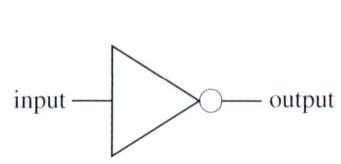

Input	Output
0	1
1	0

This has one input and one output. For the output to be ON (1), the input must NOT be ON (1).

Figure 1.21
AND, OR and NOT gates

Control in Circuits

For many practical applications more than one logic gate is needed. The gates are sometimes combined so that the output from one becomes the input of another.

Examples:

- *Car door indicator*

Figure 1.22
A car door indicator

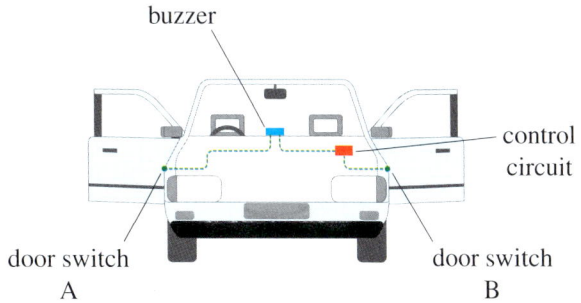

Switch A	Switch B	Buzzer
0	0	1
0	1	1
1	0	1
1	1	0

Figure 1.23
Truth table

Figure 1.24

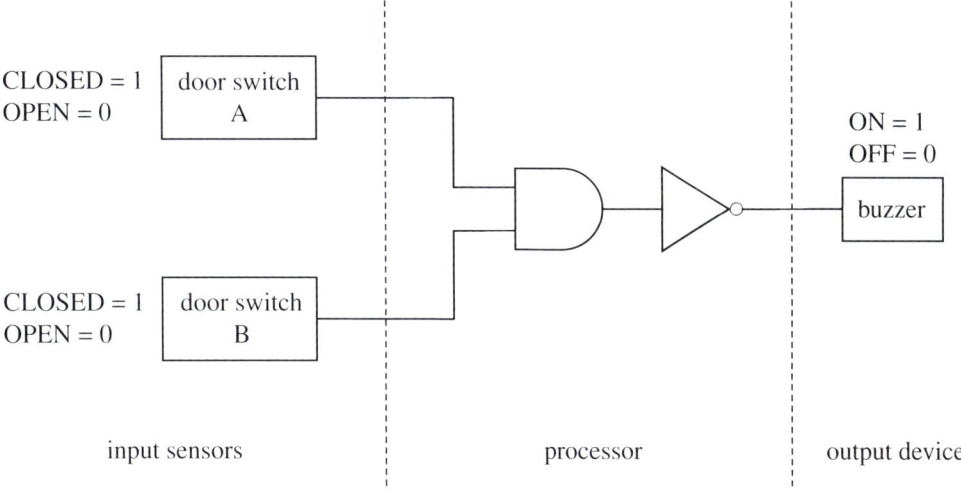

The buzzer is only OFF when both doors are closed.

- *Dawn to dusk security light*

Test switch	Light sensor	Security light
0	0	1
0	1	0
1	0	1
1	1	1

Figure 1.26
Truth table

Figure 1.25
Security light

Electricity

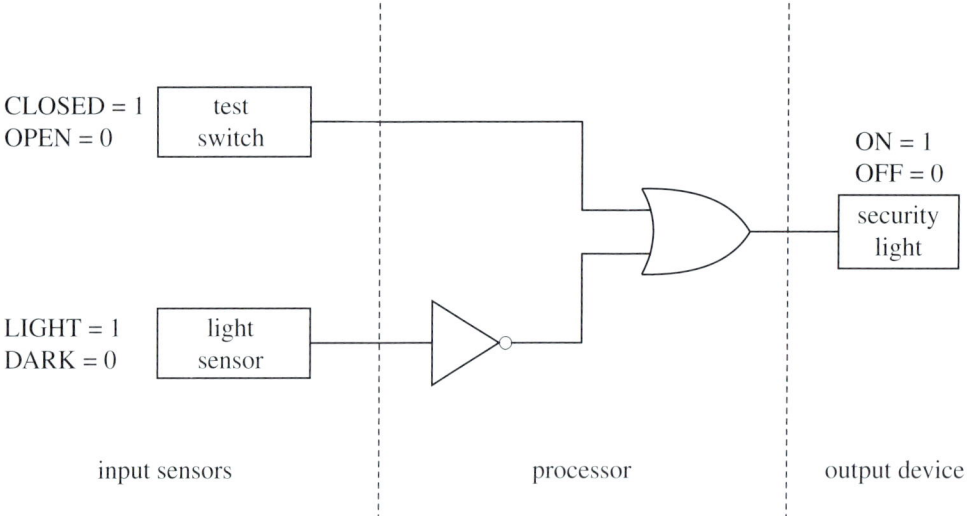

Figure 1.27 ▲

The security light will automatically switch on when it is dark. The light can be tested at any time by simply closing the test switch.

- *Automatic heater for a greenhouse*

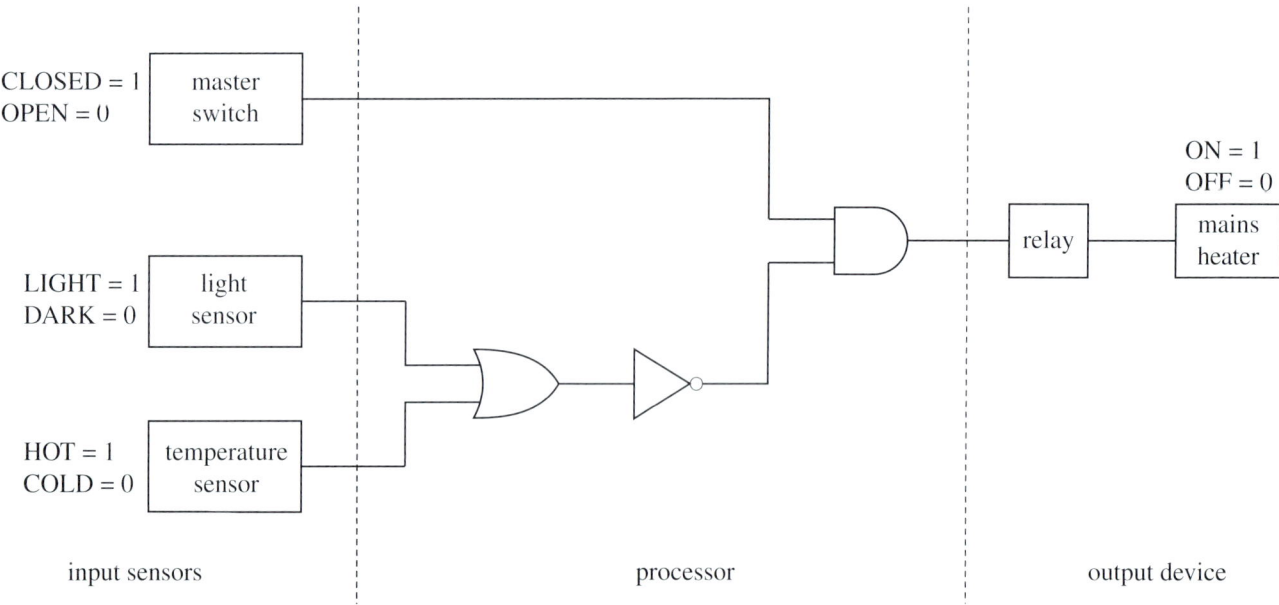

Figure 1.28 ▲

Provided the master switch is closed, the heater will automatically switch on when it is both dark and cold. The heater can be switched off at any time by opening the master switch. The AND gate cannot provide enough power to operate the heater so it switches on a relay instead. The relay switches on the separate circuit of the heater (see page 2).

Figure 1.29
A greenhouse heater

Control in Circuits

Topic questions

1. What is the difference between an AND gate and an OR gate?
2. Which of the following can be used as an output device in an electronic system?

   buzzer   heater   LDR   motor   switch   thermistor
3. Name two input sensors that could be used in a burglar alarm.
4.

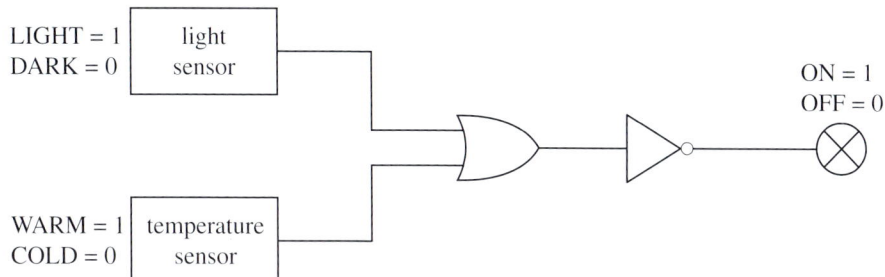

light	temperature sensor	lamp
0	0	
0	1	
1	0	

    a) Complete the truth table for the logic circuit above.
    b) Name a suitable device for use as the light sensor.
    c) Name a suitable device for use as the temperature sensor.
    d) What happens to the lamp when it is dark and cold?
    e) What happens to the lamp when it is light and warm?
    f) Suggest a practical application for this circuit.

5. The diagram below shows part of the control system for an industrial guillotine. The guillotine only works when both switches are closed at the same time.

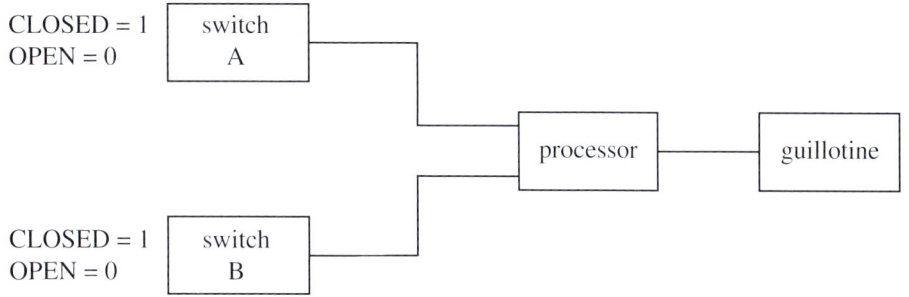

    a) Which part of the system is the output device?
    b) What type of logic gate should be used as the processor?

6. Draw the logic circuit for an alarm that will ring if either smoke or a high temperature is detected. Draw the truth table for your circuit.

Potential Divider

Two resistors joined in series can be used to split the voltage provided by a battery into two parts. Resistors used in this way form a **potential divider**. By changing the values of the resistors any fraction of the battery voltage can be obtained.

Electricity

Figure 1.30
A potential divider

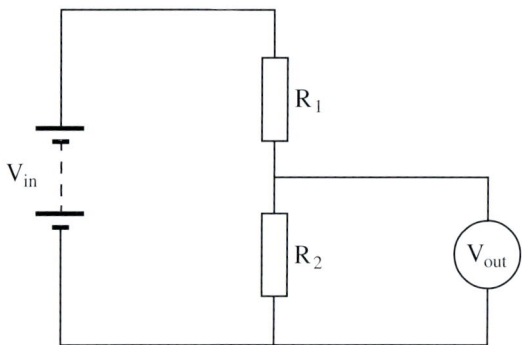

The output voltage of a potential divider can be worked out using the equation:

$$V_{out} = V_{in} \times \frac{(R_2)}{(R_1 + R_2)}$$

If either resistance R_1 or R_2 is increased (or reduced), the share of the input voltage across it also increases (or reduces).

Did you know?
The use of batteries has increased so much that more than 20 billion are sold each year.

Examples:

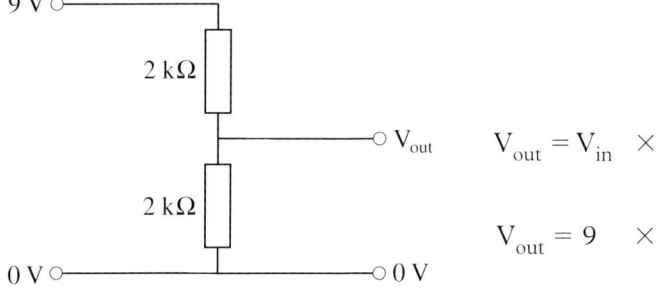

Figure 1.31

$$V_{out} = V_{in} \times \frac{(R_2)}{(R_1 + R_2)}$$

$$V_{out} = 9 \times \frac{2000}{(2000 + 2000)} = 4.5V$$

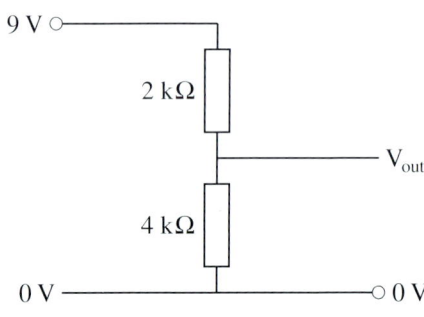

Figure 1.32

$$V_{out} = V_{in} \times \frac{(R_2)}{(R_1 + R_2)}$$

$$V_{out} = 9 \times \frac{4000}{(2000 + 4000)} = 6V$$

In control circuits an input sensor often replaces one of the resistors in the potential divider. Changes to the property that the sensor is detecting change the resistance of the sensor. This changes the value of the output voltage (V_{out}).

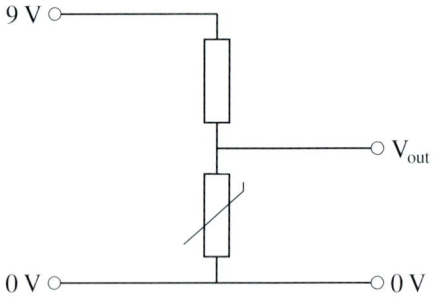

Figure 1.33

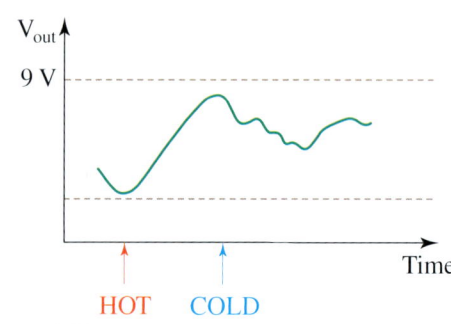

Figure 1.34
The effect of temperature on output voltage

Control in Circuits

The potential divider shown in Figure 1.33 has one fixed resistor and one thermistor. The value of the output voltage will change with temperature. When the temperature falls, the resistance of the thermistor goes up. So the share of the input voltage across the thermistor (V_{out}) goes up. V_{out} provides the input to the processor of the control circuit. If V_{out} changes enough, the input to the processor will change from being HIGH to being LOW (or from being LOW to being HIGH). In this particular circuit V_{out} could be used to switch on a heater.

It is often important that the input to the processor changes from HIGH to LOW at a particular value of the property that the sensor is detecting. For example, in a temperature control circuit a heater must switch on at a specific temperature. This can be done by using a variable resistor in place of the fixed resistor as in Figure 1.35.

Figure 1.35

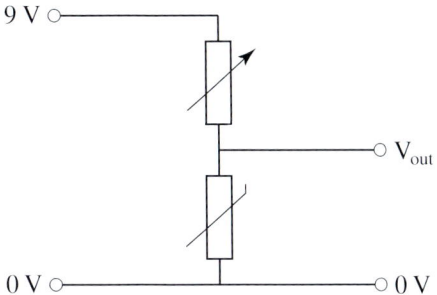

Increasing the resistance of the variable resistor causes the input to the processor to change from LOW to HIGH at a lower temperature.

Evaluating a circuit diagram

To explain how a control circuit works it is important to know what each component shown in the circuit diagram is doing.

As an example, consider the circuit shown in Figure 1.36. The circuit has been designed to work as a light dependent switch.

Figure 1.36

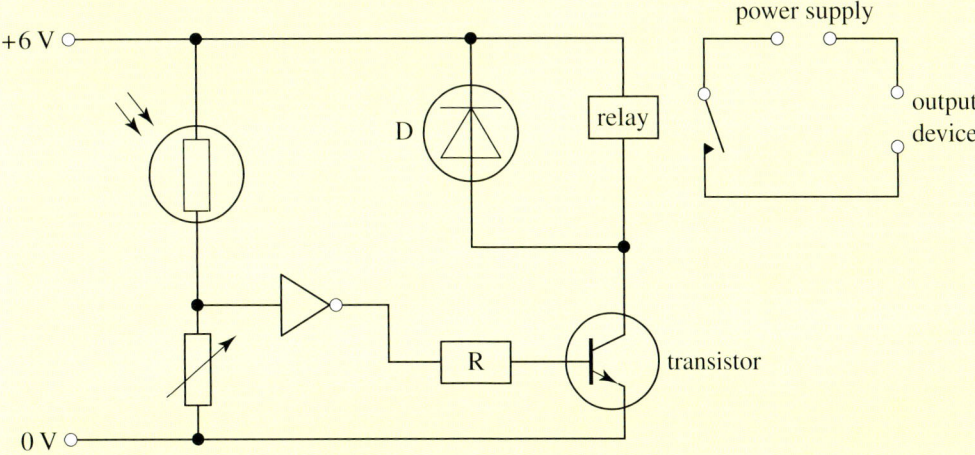

The LDR and variable resistor form a potential divider.

Since the resistance of the LDR changes with light intensity, the share of the input voltage across the LDR will change with light intensity. As it gets darker the resistance of the LDR and the voltage across the LDR go up. So the voltage across the variable resistor goes down.

13

Electricity

At some point, the input to the NOT gate will change from HIGH to LOW, causing the output from the NOT gate to change from LOW to HIGH. A small current, limited by resistor R, then flows to the transistor, which switches ON. This allows a larger current to flow through the relay coil. The relay contacts close completing the output circuit.

Adjusting the variable resistor allows the output device to be activated at different light intensities. By decreasing the resistance, the input to the NOT gate changes from HIGH to LOW at a higher light intensity. So a brighter light than previously is able to activate the output device.

The function of diode D is to protect the transistor when the relay is switched off. Without the diode a large current would flow through the transistor, which might damage it.

Swapping the position of the variable resistor and LDR causes the output device to activate as the light intensity increases from dull to bright.

Replacing the LDR with a different type of sensor would allow the circuit to be used as a different type of switch. For example, by replacing the LDR with a moisture sensor, the circuit could be used to switch on an automatic water sprinkler system.

Adding a time delay to a control circuit

Sometimes a control circuit needs to include a time delay. For example, after setting a burglar alarm the system processor allows the operator several seconds to leave the building. The output device (siren) can only be activated after this time delay.

Figure 1.37
A microwave oven switches itself off after a set time delay

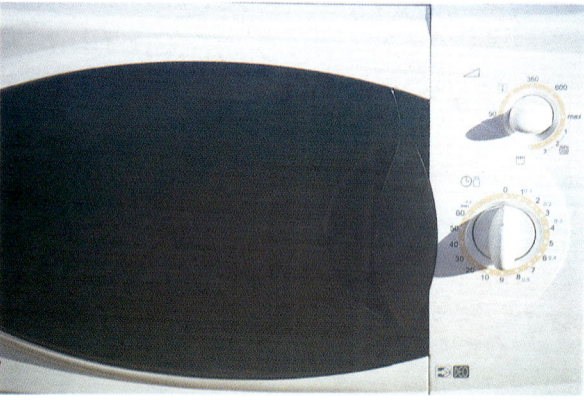

Including a **capacitor** in a circuit is one way to cause a time delay. A capacitor is a device designed to store electric charge.

Figure 1.38
Different types of capacitors

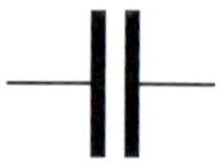

Figure 1.39
Capacitor circuit symbol

Control in Circuits

Figure 1.40 shows a circuit used to charge up a capacitor. When the switch is closed a current flows to the capacitor and charge is stored by the capacitor. The potential difference (p.d.) across the capacitor, shown by the voltmeter, increases. The reading on the voltmeter will stop going up when the capacitor is fully charged. The reading on the ammeter will drop to zero when the capacitor is fully charged.

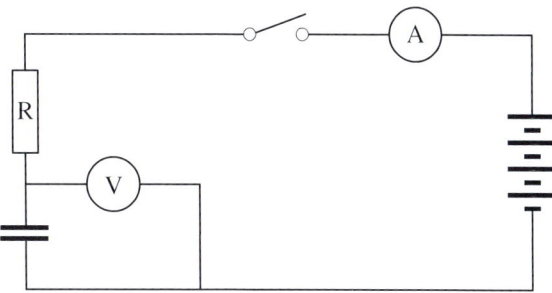

Figure 1.40

The larger the resistance of the circuit and the greater the value of the capacitor, the longer it takes for the capacitor to charge up.

Connecting a conductor across a charged capacitor causes the charge to flow away from the capacitor. The capacitor is said to be discharging. When a capacitor discharges, a current flows from the capacitor and the potential difference (p.d.) across the capacitor decreases. The capacitor is fully discharged when the p.d. across the capacitor is zero.

The greater the resistance of the discharging circuit and the greater the value of the capacitor, the longer it takes to discharge.

The rapid discharge of the capacitor in the flashgun of a camera produces a very large current for a very short time.

Figure 1.41
A camera flashgun

A time delay switch

Replacing an input sensor with a capacitor allows a time delay switch to be included in a control circuit.

Figure 1.42
A time delay switch

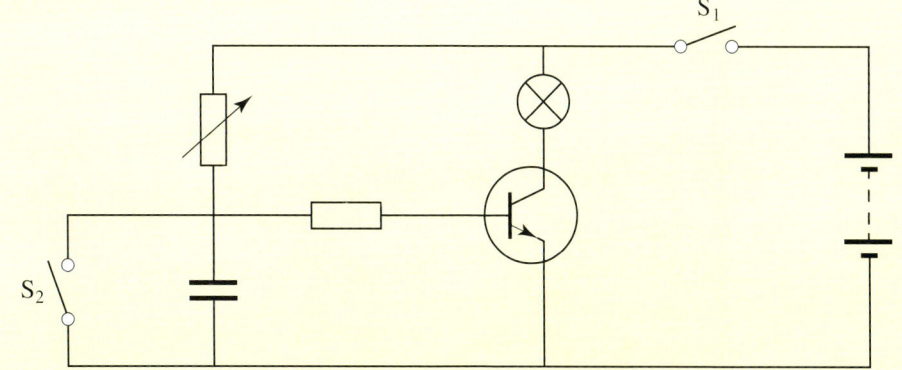

The capacitor and variable resistor form a potential divider. Closing switch S_1 (with S_2 open) causes the capacitor to charge up through the variable resistor. After a certain time the p.d. across the capacitor will have increased to the value needed to 'switch on' the transistor. Switching on the transistor completes the circuit to the lamp, so the lamp switches on.

Electricity

The time delay between closing switch S_1 and the lamp lighting up can be changed by adjusting the value of the variable resistor or by changing the value of the capacitor. Increasing the value of the variable resistor or the capacitor would increase the time delay.

Closing switch S_2 discharges the capacitor and resets the timer.

Swapping the position of the variable resistor and capacitor would make the lamp come on the moment S_1 is closed. However as the voltage across the capacitor increases, the voltage across the variable resistor decreases. After a certain time, this causes the transistor to 'switch off' and the lamp to go out.

Advantages and disadvantages of advanced electronic systems

Advanced electronic systems are having an ever-increasing impact on everyday society. Since the invention of the transistor and microchip rapid technological developments have allowed electronic systems to become smaller, faster and more sophisticated. The way we work and the way we run our lives is continually changing as a result of these technological advances. However it should be realised that the advances made to electronic systems could have both advantages and disadvantages for society and the individual. Figure 1.43 outlines some of the possible advantages and disadvantages of four widely used electronic systems.

Figure 1.43
The advantages and disadvantages of electronic systems

Electronic system	Advantages	Disadvantages
Mobile phones	• Instant communication with almost anywhere in the world. • Ability to access information 'on the move'. • Increased mobility of workforce. • Ability to call for help in an emergency.	• Possible health hazard, linked to the use of microwave radiation. • Increased levels of crime. • Visual pollution and health worries, linked to the erection of phone masts. • Reduced levels of road safety as some car drivers phone whilst driving.
Closed Circuit Television (CCTV)	• Increased levels of security. • More crimes are detected and solved.	• Relocates crime to an area without CCTV. • Invasion of privacy, you may be filmed even though you are doing nothing wrong.

A CCTV Camera

Control in Circuits

Electronic system	Advantages	Disadvantages
Robotics *A bomb disposal robot*	• Can perform many simple, dull, routine or dangerous jobs. For example, car assembly, paint spraying or bomb disposal. • Reduces human error in manufacturing and improves reliability. For example in a clothes-manufacturing factory a robotic knife can cut through many layers of material to an exact pattern. • New job opportunities in the design, manufacture and maintenance of robotic systems.	• Higher levels of unemployment in the traditional manufacturing industries. One robot may replace a large number of factory workers.
Internet	• Access to huge amounts of information and data. • Ability to go shopping without leaving your home. • Worldwide communication. • Access to services, such as banking, at any time of the day or night. • A valuable teaching and educational aid.	• The possibility of transmitting unsuitable material to adults and/or children. • Invasion of privacy, due to the storage and transmission or personal information. • Organisations are vulnerable to computer 'hackers'.

Summary

◆ A switch is one way to control a device in a circuit.

◆ The current through a circuit can be controlled using a fixed resistor or a variable resistor.

◆ Most electronic systems are designed in three parts, the input sensors, a processor and an output device.

◆ The three basic types of logic gate are called AND, OR and NOT.

◆ A potential divider can be used to split the voltage provided by a battery into two parts.

◆ A capacitor can be used in a control circuit to cause a time delay.

◆ The advances made to electronic systems can have both advantages and disadvantages for society and the individual.

Topic questions

1. Consider the circuit shown in Figure 1.36 on page 13.
   a) What changes must be made if the circuit is to switch on a fan when the temperature in a room reaches 30°C?
   b) How can the fan be made to switch on at a lower temperature?

2. Adapt the circuit shown in Figure 1.42 on page 15 so that it can be used:
   a) as an electronic egg-timer for a blind person;
   b) to switch on a 230V lamp in a photographic dark room for a set time.

Electricity

3 For each of the following circuits, calculate the value of V_{out}.

a)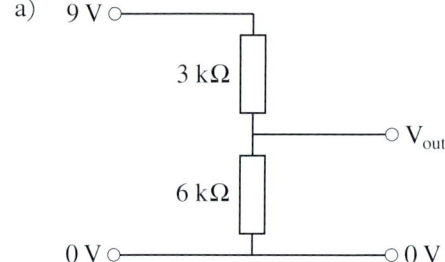

b)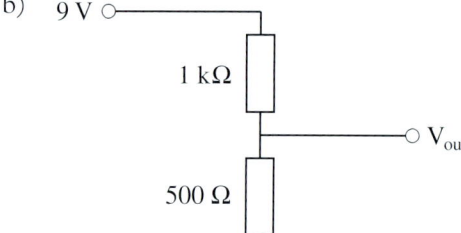

c)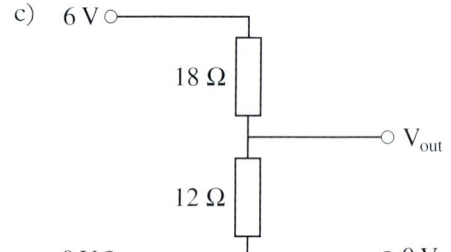

d)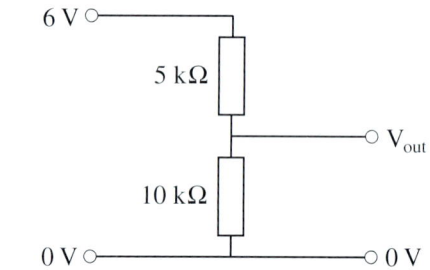

4 A capacitor is discharged through a resistor. How can the discharge time be increased?

5 Outline the reasons why some people feel that privacy is no longer possible.

6 What types of job can a robot do well and what types of job does a human worker do better?

7 Some people think that mobile phones are dangerous. Why is this?

Examination questions

1 The diagram below shows a circuit which can be used as an automatic switch.

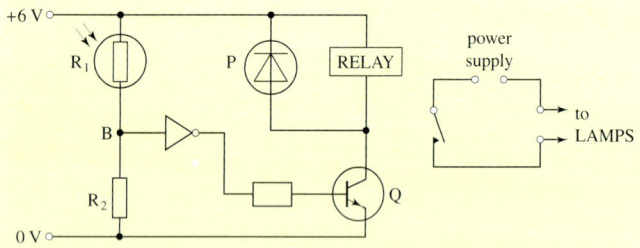

a) Name the following components: P, Q, R_1.
(3 marks)

Use the following information for parts b) and c).

$$V_{out} = V_{in} \times \frac{(R_2)}{(R_1 + R_2)}$$

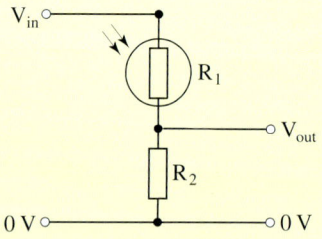

b) The resistance of R_2 = 2000Ω. V_{in} is 6V.
  i) In daylight the resistance of R_1 = 500Ω. Calculate the voltage across R_2.
  ii) In daylight the lamps will be OFF. Explain why. (6 marks)

c) In the dark the resistance of R_1 is 198000Ω. Calculate the voltage across R_2. (2 marks)

Examination questions

2 a) The diagram shows part of a simple alarm system used to protect a valuable necklace.

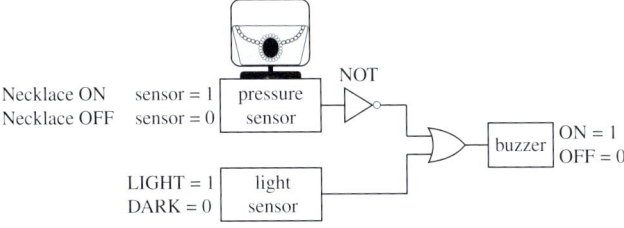

i) Copy and complete the truth table for the NOT gate.

Input	Output
1	
0	

(1 mark)

ii) Copy and complete the truth table for the alarm system.

Pressure sensor	Light sensor	Buzzer
0	0	
0	1	
1	0	
1	1	

(2 marks)

iii) Explain how this alarm system would work. *(2 marks)*

b) The alarm needs to be able to be switched on and off. To do this a key-operated switch and a logic gate **X** are added to the circuit.

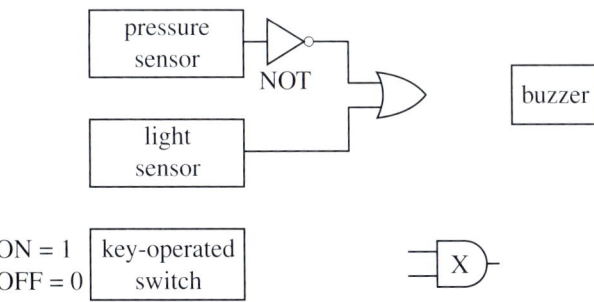

i) What type of logic gate is **X**? *(1 mark)*
ii) Copy and complete the circuit above to show how the key-operated switch and logic gate **X** should be connected into the alarm system. *(2 marks)*

3 a) The diagram shows the arrangement of the colour coded bands on a typical resistor.

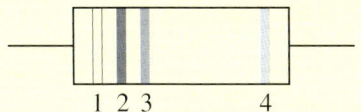

The colour code is given in the table below.

Figure	Colour
0	black
1	brown
2	red
3	orange
4	yellow
5	green
6	blue
7	violet
8	grey
9	white

i) What are the colours of the first **three** bands of a 20 kΩ resistor? *(2 marks)*
ii) What information is given by the **fourth** band? *(1 mark)*

b) The diagram shows two resistors joined in series. The variable resistor can have any value between 0 and 20 kΩ.

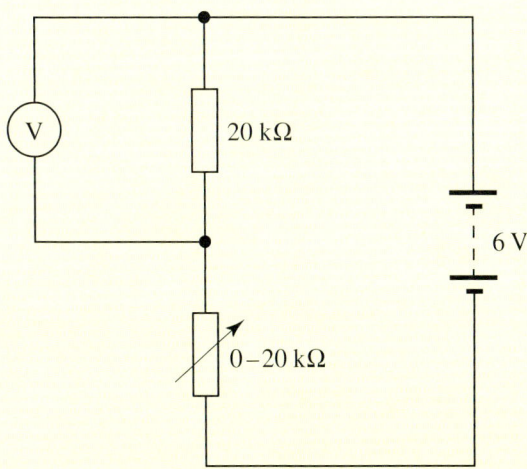

i) What is the smallest possible reading on the voltmeter? *(1 mark)*
ii) What is the largest possible reading on the voltmeter? *(1 mark)*

19

c) The diagram shows one design for a time-delay circuit.

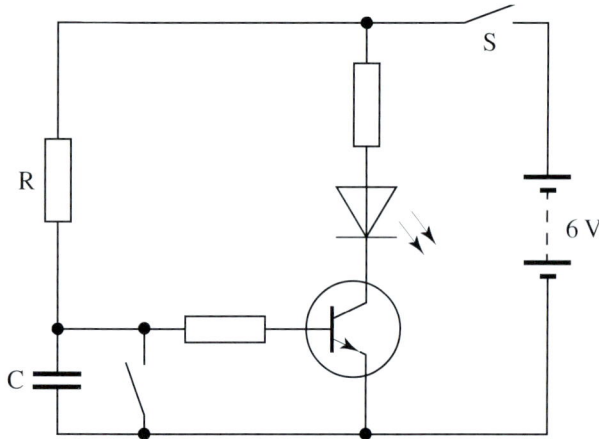

i) What is the function of a capacitor? *(1 mark)*

ii) When the switch **S** is closed, it is several minutes before the light emitting diode (LED) comes on. Explain why. The explanation has been started for you.

*When the switch **S** is closed, the voltage across the capacitor . . .* *(2 marks)*

iii) Give **one** practical use for this circuit. *(1 mark)*

iv) A pupil wires up the circuit. By mistake the positions of capacitor **C** and the resistor **R** are swapped. Describe what will happen after the switch **S** is closed. *(2 marks)*

4 In the circuit shown below all four lamps are identical.

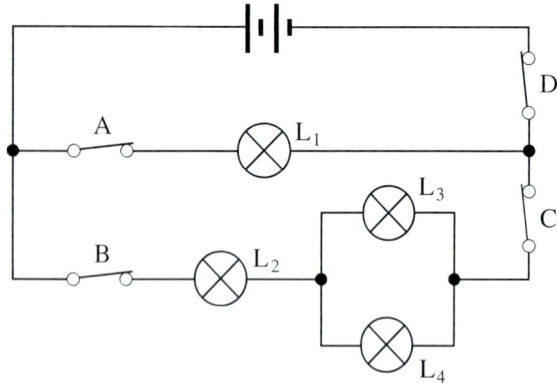

All four switches are closed (ON).
All four lamps are lit (ON).
a) Which **single** switch, **A** to **D**, should be opened in order to
i) turn OFF **all four** lamps?
ii) turn OFF one lamp only? *(2 marks)*

b) When **all four** switches are closed (ON), state which lamp L_1 to L_4 will be the brightest. Give a reason for your answer. *(2 marks)*

c) Lamps are sometimes used in electronic systems as output devices. Other devices are used as input sensors.
Below there is a list of output devices and input sensors.
Identify the **three** input sensors.

**buzzer   heater   LDR   motor
switch   thermistor**   *(3 marks)*

5 a) The diagram shows part of a heating system. It is designed to switch on automatically when it is both cold and dark. The control box contains two logic gates which are not shown.

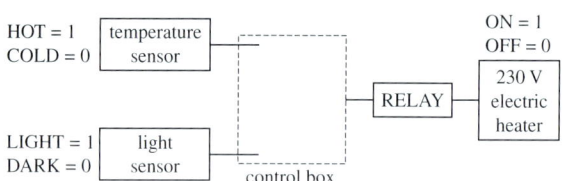

i) What is the name and circuit symbol for an input sensor which responds to light? *(2 marks)*

ii) What is the name and circuit symbol for an input sensor which responds to temperature? *(2 marks)*

iii) Copy and complete the truth table for the control system.

Light sensor	Temperature sensor	Heater
1	1	
1	0	
0	1	
0	0	

(2 marks)

iv) Identify the names of the **two** logic gates that should be used inside the control box, from the list below.
    AND   NOT   OR   *(1 mark)*

v) Copy and complete the diagram in part a) to show how the two logic gates are used to connect the input sensors to the relay. Use the correct symbols for the logic gates. *(3 marks)*

vi) Why must a relay be used to operate the heater? *(1 mark)*

b) The diagram shows an additional logic gate and switch added to the system.

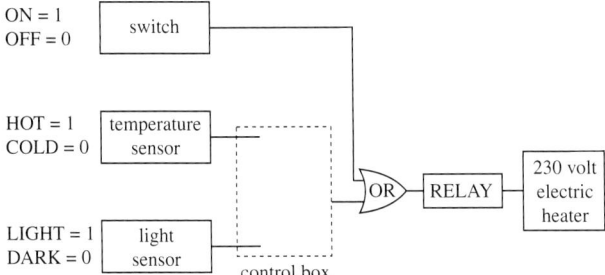

Explain how this change allows the heater to be switched on at any time. The explanation has been stared for you.

Closing the switch sends . . .   *(2 marks)*

Chapter 2
Forces and Motion

Key terms: centre of mass • centripetal force • elastic collision • kinetic energy • moment • momentum • pivot • velocity

2.1 Turning forces

Co-ordinated	Modular
10.10	15.1 15.2 mod 24

To undo a tight nut using just fingers is difficult. The job is made much easier if a spanner is used. The same force will then give a much larger turning effect. The longer the spanner, the larger the turning effect because the force will be further from the turning point or **pivot**.

Figure 2.1

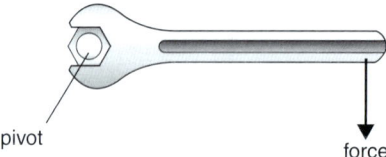

The size of the turning effect about a pivot is called the **moment**. A moment can be worked out using the following equation:

moment = force × perpendicular distance between line
(in newton-metres) (in newtons)   of action and pivot
(in metres)

Moments are usually measured in newton-metres, this can be written as Nm. Figure 2.2 shows how the perpendicular distance between the line of action of the force and pivot is measured.

Figure 2.2
Measuring perpendicular distance

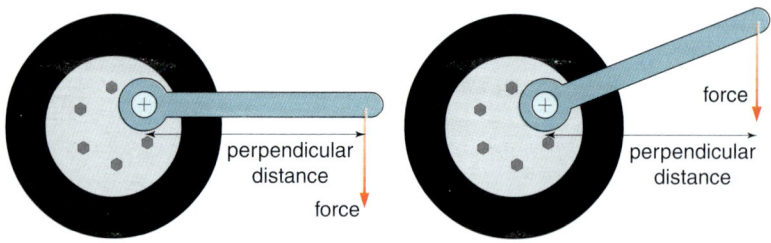

Turning Forces

Figure 2.3

The person in Figure 2.3 is pushing the door as hard as possible, but it's not closing. This is because the person is pushing at the hinge and the hinge is the pivot. The distance between the force and the pivot is zero, so the moment is zero.

Example: Calculate the moment exerted by the cyclist in Figure 2.4 on the pedal.

$$\text{force} = 120 \text{ newtons (N)}$$
$$\text{distance} = 0.2 \text{ metres (m)}$$
$$\text{moment} = ?$$

moment = force × perpendicular distance between line of action and pivot

moment = 120 × 0.2 = 24 newton metres (Nm)

Figure 2.4

Figure 2.5 shows two children on a playground see-saw.

Figure 2.5

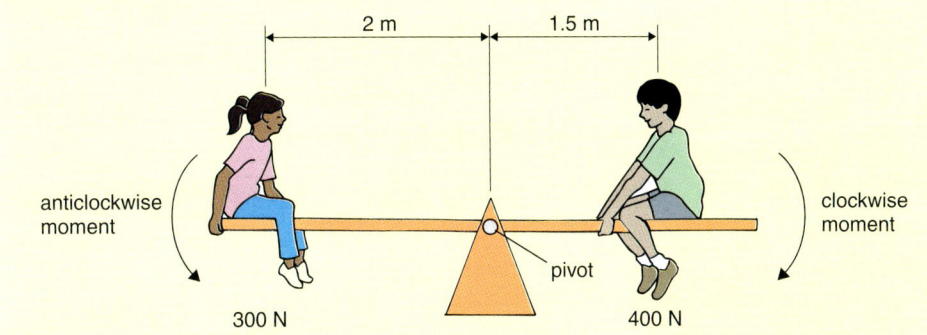

The moment of the boy is trying to turn the see-saw clockwise. The moment of the girl is trying to turn the see-saw anticlockwise. But the see-saw is not turning – it is balanced (in equilibrium). This means that the size of the clockwise moment must be the same as the size of the anticlockwise moment.

When an object is not turning:

total clockwise moment = total anticlockwise moment

Lots of joints in the human body act as pivots. Your elbow joint acts as a pivot, it lets your lower arm rotate up towards your shoulder and down towards your leg. Holding your lower arm horizontal will soon make your bicep muscle ache. This is because the clockwise moment produced by the weight of your lower arm must be balanced by an anticlockwise moment from the biceps muscle. Figure 2.7 shows the forces acting on your lower arm when you hold it horizontal.

23

Forces and Motion

Figure 2.6 ▲

clockwise moment produced by the lower arm = 15 × 0.20
= 3 Nm

anticlockwise moment produced by the biceps muscle = F × 0.05

total clockwise moment = total anticlockwise moment

3 = F × 0.05

F = force in the biceps muscle = 60 N

So the force exerted by the muscle to hold the lower arm horizontal is four times larger than the weight of the lower arm itself. This is because the muscle is attached so close to the pivot.

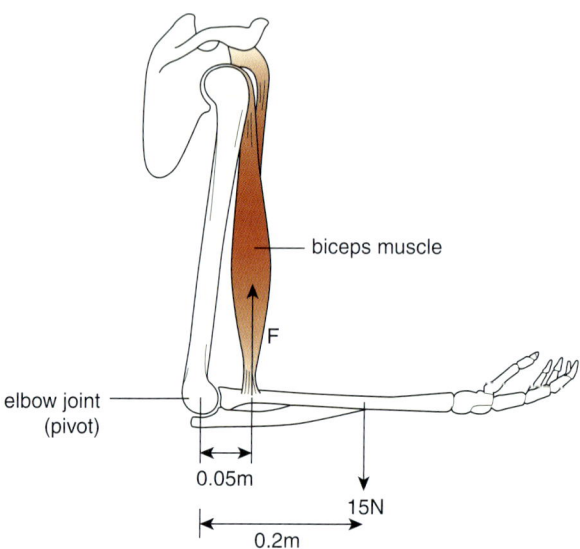

Figure 2.7 ▶

Centre of mass

Balancing a ruler on the tip of a finger is easy. But it only works if the centre of the ruler rests on the finger tip.

Figure 2.8

This balance point on the ruler is called the **centre of mass**. Although every part of the ruler has a mass, the centre of mass is the point where all the mass of the ruler can be thought to be concentrated. This is also the point through which the weight of the ruler acts (the centre of gravity). So if the finger tip (the pivot) is positioned at the centre of mass, the weight of the ruler will produce no clockwise or anticlockwise moment, the ruler is therefore balanced.

Turning Forces

A tightrope walker will stay balanced if he keeps his centre of mass directly above the rope. The long pole helps the tight rope walker to keep his balance. If he starts to topple to one side of the rope, moving the pole to the other side will bring the centre of mass of the walker and the pole back over the rope.

Figure 2.9
A tightrope walker

The ruler in Figure 2.8 is symmetrical. The centre of mass of the ruler is at the centre of the ruler, along an axis of symmetry.

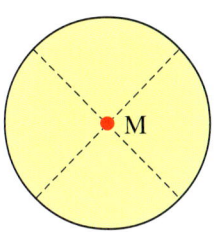
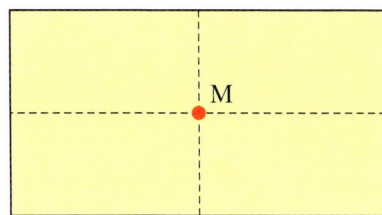

Figure 2.10 shows three common symmetrical shapes. The dotted lines are axes of symmetry.

For all symmetrical objects, the centre of mass (M) is along an axis of symmetry.

Figure 2.10 ▲

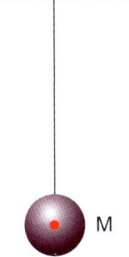

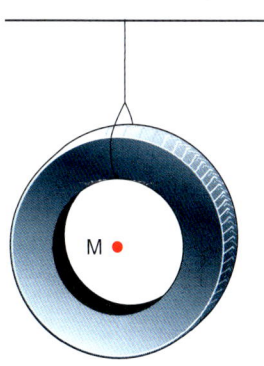

Figure 2.11 ▶

When an object is suspended it will come to rest with its centre of mass directly below the point of suspension. This is why a plumb-line always hangs vertically.

The centre of mass of an object is not always within the object itself. The centre of mass of the tyre in Figure 2.11 is in the air at the centre of the circle. But the tyre is still balanced.

Figure 2.12
A decorator using a plumb line

25

Forces and Motion

Did you know?

The men's world pole-vaulting record of 6.14 metres was set in 1994 by Sergey Bubka from the Ukraine. Pole-vaulting is a new sport for women. The women's world record stands at 4.62 metres, set in 2000 by Stacey Draglia of the USA.

By arching their back pole-vaulters can move their centres of mass outside their body. This lets them jump higher. The energy they use to lift themselves off the ground raises their centre of mass which passes under the bar. But their body passes over the bar.

Figure 2.13
Sergey Bubka in action

Finding a centre of mass

The centre of mass of an irregularly shaped piece of card can be found using a plumb-line. First a small hole is made in the card. The card is then suspended from a long pin. The card must be able to swing freely. A plumb-line is also suspended from the pin. When the card stops swinging, a line showing the position of the plumb-line is drawn on the card. The centre of mass of the card must be somewhere along this line. The card is now suspended from a different point. The plumb-line is used to draw a second vertical line. Where the two lines cross is the centre of mass of the card.

Figure 2.14
Finding the centre of mass

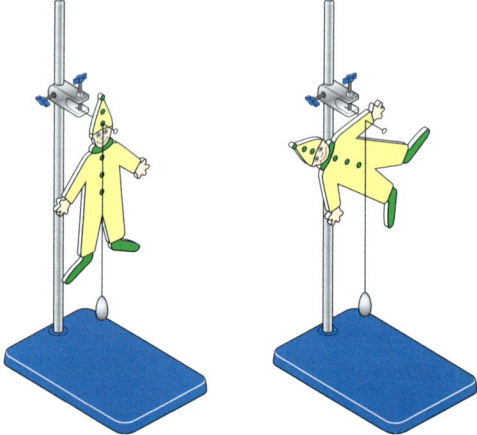

If the position of the centre of mass is accurate the card will balance at this point on the tip of a finger.

Figure 2.15

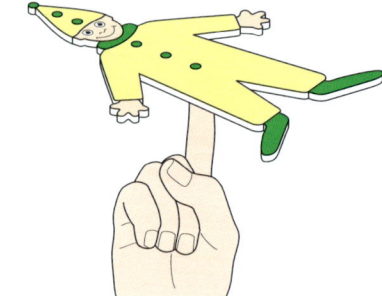

Turning Forces

An object with a pivot not passing through its centre of mass will always try to turn. But the object can be balanced using an additional force. Imagine a window cleaner walking along carrying a ladder on his shoulder. A bucket of water hangs from one end of the ladder. The weight of the ladder (acting at the centre of mass of the ladder) causes an anticlockwise moment. But the ladder and bucket of water are balanced so there must be an equal clockwise moment. The weight of the bucket of water causes the clockwise moment.

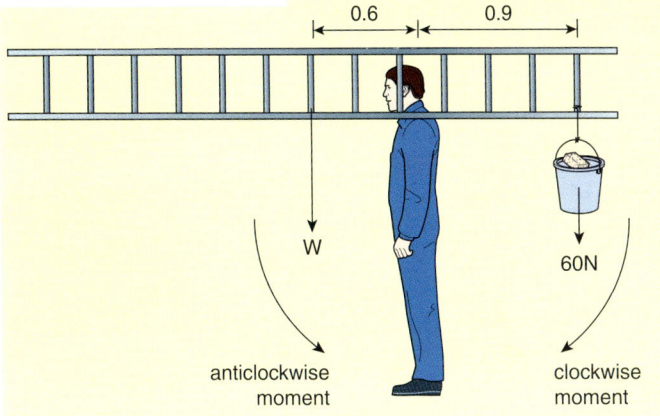

clockwise moment = 60 × 0.9

= 54 Nm

anticlockwise moment = W × 0.6

clockwise moment = anticlockwise moment

54 = W × 0.6

W = 90 N

Figure 2.16

Stability

Most objects are designed to be stable. This means that if they are tilted slightly and then released they will not fall over. They will fall back to their original position. If tilted too much the object will become unstable and fall over. So how much can an object be tilted and still be stable. Figure 2.17 shows two different table lamps. The vertical lines drawn from the centres of mass show the line of action of the weight of each lamp.

Figure 2.17

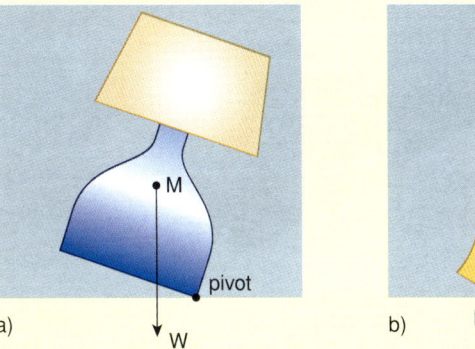
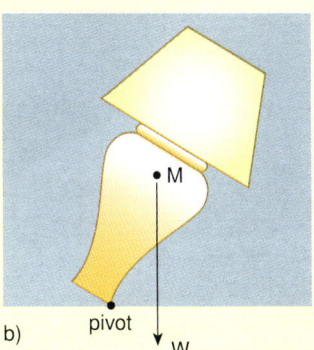

In Figure 2.17a, the line of action of the weight falls inside the base of the lamp. The lamp will fall back to its original position, it is stable. In Figure 2.17b, the line of action of the weight falls outside the base of the lamp. The turning effect now caused by the weight makes the lamp topple over. The lamp is unstable.

Forces and Motion

Figure 2.19
A tractor ploughing a hillside

Figure 2.18

Tractors are often used on sloping ground, so stability is an important part of their design. Stability is achieved by having a low centre of mass and a wide wheel base. Figure 2.18 shows that even on sloping ground the line of action of the weight falls within the wheel base of the tractor, so the tractor is stable.

Did you know?

Speed skiers can exceed 160 km/hr. At this speed stability is very important.

Figure 2.20
A speed skier in action

Summary

- A moment can be worked out using the equation:

    moment = force × perpendicular distance between line of action and pivot

- When an object is not turning, the total clockwise moment equals the total anticlockwise moment.

- The centre of mass is the point where all the mass of an object can be thought to be concentrated.

- If the line of action of the weight of an object lies outside the base of the object, the object will tend to fall over, it is unstable.

Turning Forces

Topic questions

1. Copy and complete the following sentences:
   a) The turning effect of a force is also called its _____ .
   b) A suspended object will come to rest with its _____ of _____ directly below the point of _____ .
   c) When an object is balanced, the total _____ moments must be _____ to the total _____ moments.

2. A person is trying to lever a nail out of a block of wood using a claw hammer. Why will the nail come out more easily if a hammer with a longer shaft is used?

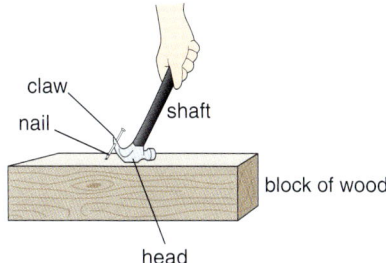

3. The diagram shows a spanner being used to undo a tight nut. Calculate the size of the turning moment exerted by the force on the nut.

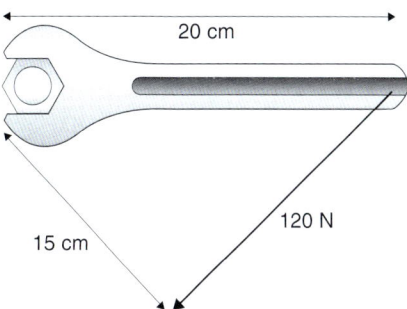

4. The diagram shows two children playing on a see-saw. If the see-saw is balanced what is the value of X?

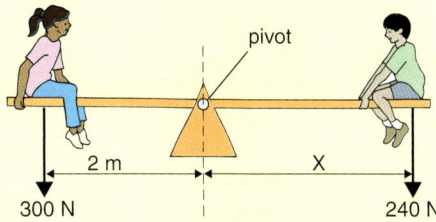

5. A crane is used to lift a container off a ship. Calculate the weight of the counterbalance needed to stop the crane from falling over.

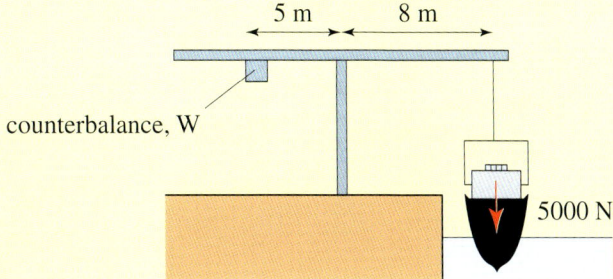

Did you know?

The tallest mobile crane can lift a weight of 300 000 newtons to a height of 160 metres.

29

6 A builder needs to weigh a symmetrical plank of wood. The maximum range of the builders spring balance is less than the weight of the plank. The diagram shows how the builder overcame this problem.

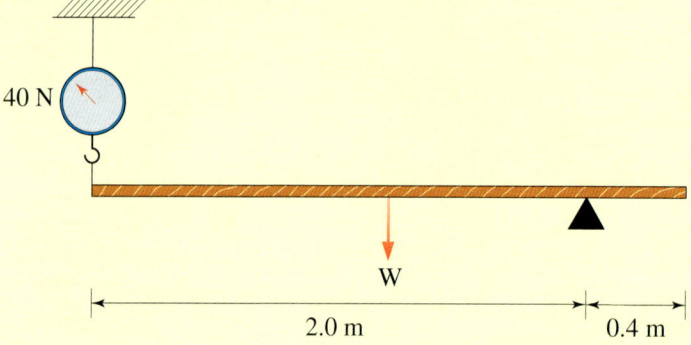

Calculate the weight of the plank.

7 The diagram shows a student leaning back on her stool. The stool and student are about to topple over.

a) Which one of the dots, A, B or C marks the centre of mass of the stool and student? Explain the reason for your choice.
b) How could the stool have been designed to make it more stable?

8 The diagram shows a simple balancing toy.

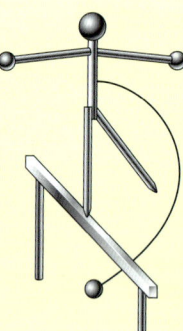

Given a small push the toy will rock backwards and forwards without falling off the bar. Explain why.

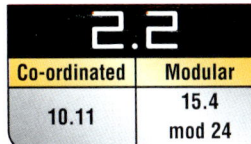

Momentum

2.2 Momentum

Co-ordinated 10.11 | Modular 15.4 mod 24

A moving object has both **kinetic energy** and **momentum**. The greater the mass of the object and the faster it moves, the more kinetic energy and momentum it has. In some situations it is more useful to consider the momentum of an object rather than its kinetic energy.

The momentum of an object is defined by the equation:

$$\text{momentum (in kilogram metre/second)} = \text{mass (in kilograms)} \times \text{velocity (in metres/second)}$$

The unit of momentum, kilogram metre/second, is usually written as kg m/s.

Just like **velocity**, momentum has both a magnitude (size) and a direction. The momentum of an object is always in the same direction as the velocity of the object. So if two objects move in opposite directions one will have positive momentum and the other negative momentum.

Figure 2.21
A charging rhino has lots of momentum

Example: A lorry and a car are travelling in opposite directions. Calculate the momentum of each vehicle.

Figure 2.22

	Lorry	
mass	=	5500 kg
velocity	=	14 m/s to the right
momentum	=	mass × velocity
	=	5500 × 14
	=	77 000 kg m/s
momentum of the lorry	=	+ 77 000 kg m/s

	Car	
mass	=	800 kg
velocity	=	25 m/s to the left
momentum	=	mass × velocity
	=	800 × 25
	=	20 000 kg m/s
momentum of the car	=	− 20 000 kg m/s

The momentum of the lorry moving to the right has been taken to be positive, so the momentum of the car moving to the left must be given as negative.

Forces and Motion

Force and momentum

When a resultant force acts on an object, the object will accelerate. This means that the velocity, and therefore the momentum, of the object will change. So a resultant force acting on an object will cause a change in momentum.

The size of the resultant force and the change in momentum that occurs are linked by the following equation:

$$\text{force (in newtons)} = \frac{\text{change in momentum (in kilogram metre/second)}}{\text{time (in seconds)}}$$

A small force acting for a long time can cause the same change in momentum as a large force acting for a small time.

Golf and cricket are just two of the sports that demonstrate momentum.

Figure 2.23
A golfer follows through to give the ball more momentum

The golfer swings the club, hits the ball and follows through. The follow through means that the club does not stop the moment it hits the ball. The club continues, for a short time, to move with the ball. This action increases the time that the force acts on the ball, which increases the change in momentum of the ball. So the ball will move faster and travel further.

Figure 2.24
A cricketer draws his hands back to reduce the impact of the ball

Catching a fast moving cricket ball can be a painful experience. Using a large force to stop the ball quickly will produce an equally large force on the catcher's hands.

By pulling his hands backwards as he catches the ball, the cricketer takes longer to reduce the momentum of the ball to zero. This reduces both the force needed to stop the ball and the force exerted on the cricketer's hands.

Momentum

Figure 2.25

Example: The picture shows a golfer about to strike a stationary golf ball of mass 0.045 kilogrammes.

When the golf club strikes the ball it is in contact for 0.001 seconds and exerts a force of 3600 newtons on the ball. Calculate the velocity at which the ball leaves the club.

$$\text{change in momentum} = \text{force} \times \text{time}$$
$$= 3600 \times 0.001$$
$$= 3.6 \text{ kg m/s}$$

since the ball was initially stationary,

$$\text{change in momentum} = \text{mass} \times \text{final velocity}$$

$$\text{So, final velocity} = \frac{\text{change in momentum}}{\text{mass}} = \frac{3.6}{0.045} = 80 \text{ m/s}$$

Momentum and safety

When an object collides with another, the two objects exert a force on each other. These forces are equal in size, but opposite in direction. The change in momentum of each object will be equal in size, but opposite in direction. The longer the time of contact the smaller the force needed to change the momentum. This is the principle behind many different types of safety devices.

Figure 2.26

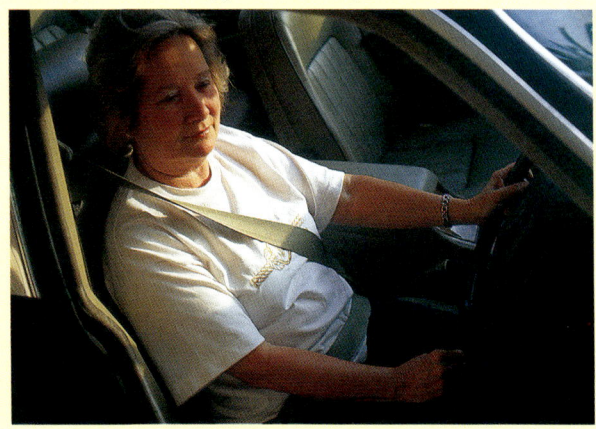

A seat belt is not rigid. In a crash it is designed to stretch slightly. This is very important, since it increases the time taken for the momentum of the passenger to be reduced to zero. So both the force on the passenger's body and the subsequent risk of injury are reduced.

Forces and Motion

Figure 2.27

The helmet worn by a cyclist and the body protector worn by a horse rider work in the same way. If the cyclist falls off and hits his/her head, the padding inside the helmet will start to crush.

Figure 2.28

If the horse rider falls off, the padding inside the body protector will start to crush. In both cases the time taken to stop has been increased so reducing the force on the rider.

Collisions and explosions

In any collision or explosion, the momentum after the collision or explosion in a particular direction, is the same as the momentum in that direction before the collision or explosion.

That is:

$$\text{total momentum after a collision or explosion} = \text{total momentum before a collision or explosion}$$

Momentum is conserved provided there are no external forces acting.

Collisions

Consider the white snooker ball in Figure 2.29 moving with velocity 'v' directly towards a red snooker ball. Before they collide the red ball is not moving. The red ball has zero momentum.

Figure 2.29

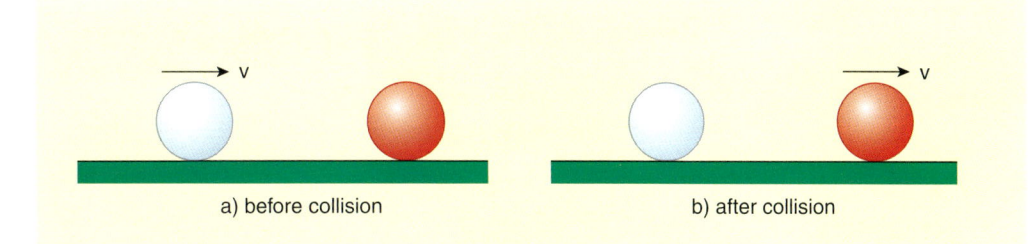

a) before collision

b) after collision

During the collision, an equal size force will act on each ball, but in opposite directions. The forces will also act for the same time. The momentum of each ball will therefore change by the same amount.

(*Remember*: force × time = change in momentum)

After the collision the white ball will be stationary. The white ball has zero momentum. The red ball will move with a velocity 'v' in the same direction as the white ball was moving. The total momentum after the collision is the same as the total momentum before the collision.

Momentum has been conserved, but what of kinetic energy?

(*Remember*: kinetic energy = ½ × mass × velocity²)

Before the collision only the white ball has kinetic energy. After the collision only the red ball has kinetic energy. The velocities before and after the collision are the same. So the total kinetic energy before and after the collision is the same. This is an **elastic collision**. Elastic collisions are those that involve no overall change in kinetic energy.

Most collisions are not perfectly elastic. Usually when objects collide, the total kinetic energy after the collision is less than before the collision. Some of the kinetic energy is transferred to other forms of energy.

Explosions

An explosion is the opposite of a collision. Instead of moving together, objects move apart. But like a collision, the total momentum of the objects involved in an explosion remains constant. In an explosion momentum is conserved.

Example: At the 'Circus on Ice' a clown throws a 'custard pie' forwards with as much force as possible. Before throwing the pie, the clown was not moving.

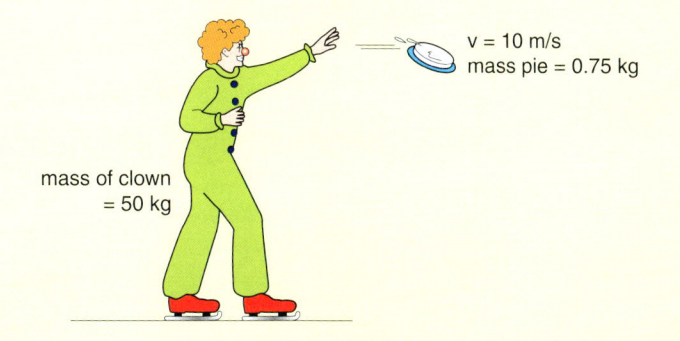

Figure 2.30

v = 10 m/s
mass pie = 0.75 kg

mass of clown
= 50 kg

Calculate the speed at which the clown moves backwards.

35

Forces and Motion

The total momentum of the clown and pie before throwing = 0

Momentum of clown and pie before throwing = Momentum of clown and pie after throwing

$$0 = \underset{\text{of the pie}}{\text{Forward momentum}} + \underset{\text{of the clown}}{\text{backward momentum}}$$

$$0 = (0.75 \times 10) + (50 \times v)$$

$$0 = 7.5 + (50 \times v)$$

$$v = -0.15 \text{ m/s}$$

The negative sign means that the clown does move in the opposite direction to the pie.

Figure 2.31
The launch of a space shuttle

The principle of momentum conservation is used in the launch of a space shuttle. Before the launch the total momentum of the shuttle and fuel is zero. After lift off the total momentum must still be zero. So the downward momentum of the hot exhaust gases must be equal to the upward momentum of the shuttle.

Summary

- Momentum is defined by the equation:

  $$\text{momentum} = \text{mass} \times \text{velocity}$$

- The unit of momentum is the kilogram metre/second (kg m/s).
- Momentum has both magnitude (size) and direction.

- $$\text{force} = \frac{\text{change in momentum}}{\text{time}}$$

- total momentum after a = total momentum before
  collision or explosion   a collision or explosion
  (provided no external forces act)

- Elastic collisions are those that involve no overall change in kinetic energy.

Circular Motion

Topic questions

1. Copy and complete the following sentences:
   a) An object that is not moving has _____ momentum.
   b) Momentum, like velocity has both _____ and _____ .
   c) Momentum is worked out by multiplying _____ and _____ .

2. Work out the momentum of:
   a) a jogger of mass 75 kg running at 3 m/s.
   b) a cyclist of mass 60 kg peddling at 8 m/s
   c) a hockey ball of mass 0.5 kg moving at 12 m/s
   d) a bullet of mass 10 g moving at 250 m/s

3. A racing car, travelling at 85 m/s, has a momentum of 42 500 kg m/s. What is the mass of the racing car?

4. An elephant of mass 1800 kg has a momentum of 10 800 kg m/s. How fast is the elephant moving?

5. During a crash test, a car of mass 840 kg is driven into a wall at 5 m/s. The car slows down and stops in 1.5 seconds. Calculate the force on the car during the collision.

6. A trolley of mass 2 kg, travelling at 3 m/s, collides with a stationary 1 kg trolley. If the trolleys stick together, calculate:
   a) the total momentum before the collision,
   b) the speed of the two trolleys after the collision.

7. Explain how the speed of a rocket travelling through space can be increased.

8. A bullet is fired into a block of wood. The collision is not elastic. Explain why.

2.3 Circular motion

Co-ordinated	Modular
10.12	15.3 mod 24

Figure 2.32
A skydiver falls with a constant velocity

Figure 2.32 shows the forces acting on a skydiver. The two forces are equal in size and opposite in direction. So the forces are balanced.

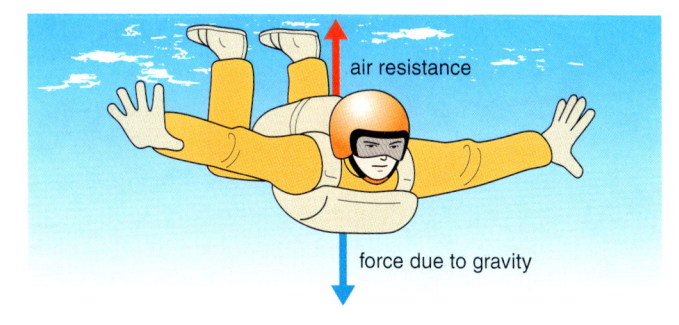

Balanced forces do not change the velocity of an object, so the skydiver will fall at a constant speed in a straight line. But objects do not always move in straight lines, sometimes they follow circular paths. This means that they are continually changing direction. But when the direction changes, the velocity of the object changes. For this to happen a resultant, unbalanced force is needed.

37

Forces and Motion

Figure 2.33

A ball can be tied to a piece of string and whirled around in a horizontal circle.

The speed of the ball stays the same but its direction is constantly changing. So its velocity is also changing. The force that causes the change in velocity is the inward pull of the string on the ball. This force is always towards the centre of the circle, at right angles to the direction the ball is travelling in. The force does not increase or decrease the speed of the ball. If the string breaks the ball would fly off in a straight line in the direction of travel, as in Figure 2.34.

Figure 2.34

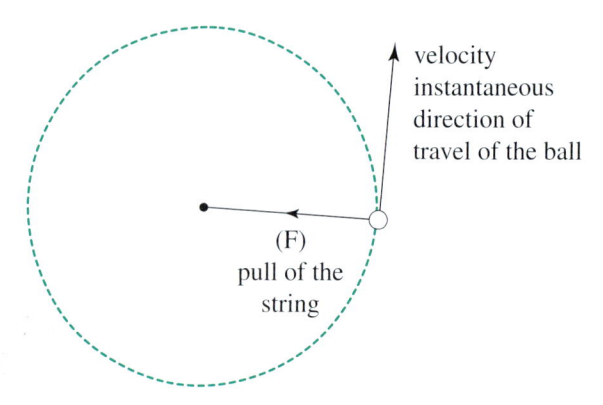

velocity
instantaneous direction of travel of the ball

(F) pull of the string

The same idea is used in the sport of hammer throwing. The athlete makes the hammer move in a circle by using the pull of their arms. At the right moment the athlete lets go and the hammer flies off into the air.

Figure 2.35
A hammer thrower

Did you know?

The men's world hammer throwing record of 86.7 metres was set by Yuriy Sedykh in 1986.

Circular Motion

The resultant force that makes an object move in a circle is called the **centripetal force**. This force always acts inwards, towards the centre of the circle. Although a centripetal force can be provided in different ways, the size of the centripetal force always depends upon the same three factors. The centripetal force is greater:

- the greater the mass of the object;
- the greater the speed of the object;
- the smaller the radius of the circle.

The speed of the object has the greatest effect on the size of the centripetal force. If speed doubles, the centripetal force increases four times.

Centripetal force in action

There must be a centripetal force on a motorbike when it goes around a bend in the road. This force is provided by the friction between the road and the motorbike's tyres. Ice on the road will reduce the friction. A motorcyclist must reduce speed if they want to stay in control and not skid off the road.

Figure 2.36
A motorcyclist taking a corner at high speed

Figure 2.37
A satellite orbiting the Earth

Many satellites move in circular orbits around the Earth. The centripetal force is provided by the gravitational pull of the Earth on the satellite. In a similar way the Earth is kept in orbit around the Sun by a centripetal force. In this case the force is provided by the gravitational pull of the Sun on the Earth.

Did you know?
Satellites orbiting close to the Earth have speeds of about 29 000 km/hr.

Forces and Motion

Figure 2.38

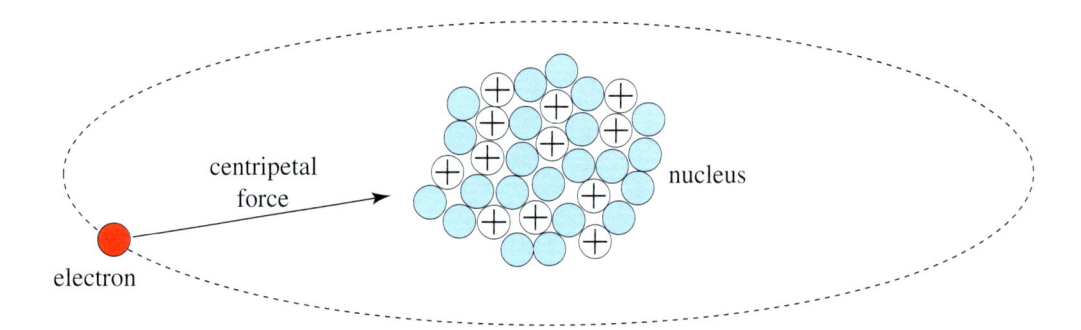

For electrons to orbit the nucleus of an atom there must be a centripetal force. The force is provided by the electrostatic attraction between the negative electron and the positive nucleus.

Summary

♦ Any object moving in a circle is acted on by a centripetal force.

♦ The centripetal force on an object is affected by the mass of the object, the speed of the object and the radius of the object's circular path.

Topic questions

1. Copy and complete the following sentences.
   a) The _____ force needed when a car travels around a bend in the road is provided by the force of _____ between the road and the car _____ .
   b) The force keeping the Moon in orbit around the Earth is the _____ pull of the _____ on the Moon.
   c) The faster a bicycle is ridden around a corner in the road the _____ the centripetal _____ acting on it.

2. Explain how an object can stay at a constant speed and at the same time change its velocity.

3. The photograph shows a space station in orbit around the Earth.

   What happens to the centripetal force if:
   i) the mass of the space station increases;
   ii) the space station is moved into an orbit further from the Earth?

Examination questions

4. Under normal conditions the maximum speed that a lorry can go around a bend without skidding is 60 km/hr. Would the lorry be able to go around the bend faster, at the same speed, or would it need to slow down, if the road was muddy? Explain the reason for your answer.

Examination questions

1. The diagram shows a spanner being used to undo a tight nut.

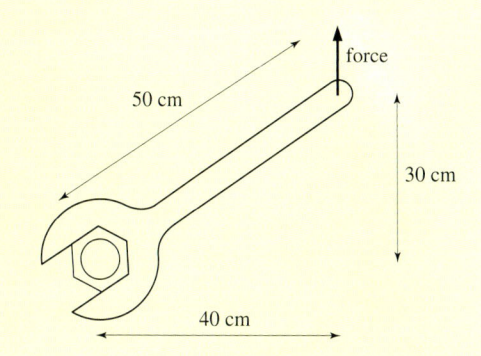

   The nut was tightened using a moment of 120 newton metres.

   Use the following equation to calculate the force needed to undo the nut. Show clearly how you work out your answer.

   moment = force × perpendicular distance from pivot

   (2 marks)

2. The diagram shows a tower crane.

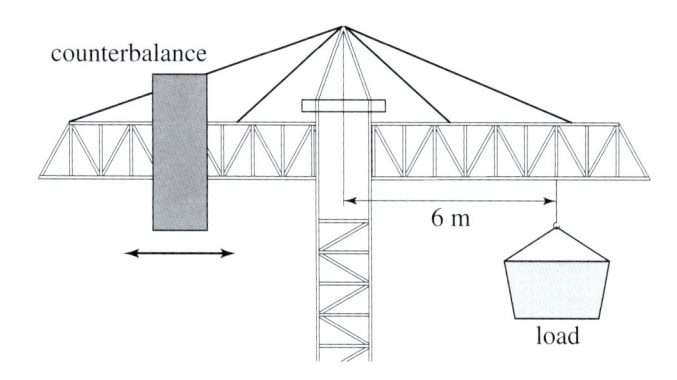

   a) Explain why the crane would be unstable without the counterbalance. *(2 marks)*
   b) The counterbalance can be moved to the left or right, as shown by the arrows on the diagram. Explain the advantage of having a movable counterbalance. *(2 marks)*
   c) The load shown in the diagram is 75 000N. The load is 6 m from the tower. Calculate the turning effect (moment) of the load in newton metres. *(2 marks)*
   d) The crane is balanced and horizontal. What is the turning effect (moment) of the counterbalance in newton metres? Explain your answer.
   (3 marks)

3. a) A thin sheet of cardboard is cut to the shape below. Describe, with a diagram, an experiment to find its centre of mass.

   (5 marks)

   b) Copy and label with an **X** the centre of mass of each of the three objects below.

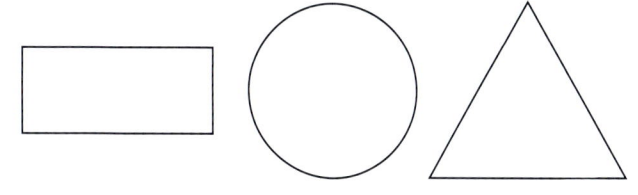

   (3 marks)

   c) Explain why a mechanic would choose a long spanner to undo a tight nut. *(2 marks)*

4. a) The diagram shows three aeroplanes at an airport.

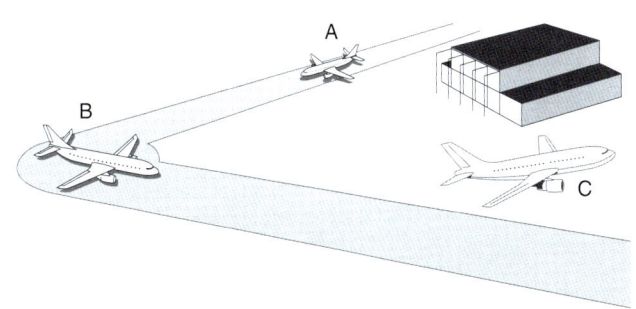

   Aeroplane **A** is moving at constant velocity towards the main runway.
   Aeroplane **B** is stationary, waiting to take off.
   Aeroplane **C** has just taken off and is accelerating.

i) Which, if any, of the aeroplanes has zero momentum? *(1 mark)*
ii) The momentum of **one** of the aeroplanes is changing. Which one? Give a reason for your answer. *(2 marks)*

5 The picture shows luggage which has been loaded onto a conveyor belt.

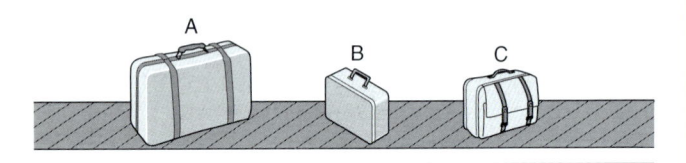

Each piece of luggage has a different mass.
mass of **A** = 22 kg
mass of **B** = 12 kg
mass of **C** = 15 kg

a) i) What is the momentum of the luggage before the conveyor belt starts to move? Give a reason for your answer. *(2 marks)*
ii) When the conveyor belt is switched on the luggage moves with a constant speed. Which piece of luggage **A**, **B** or **C** has the most momentum? Give a reason for your answer. *(2 marks)*
iii) At one point the conveyor belt turns left. The luggage on the belt continues to move at a constant speed.

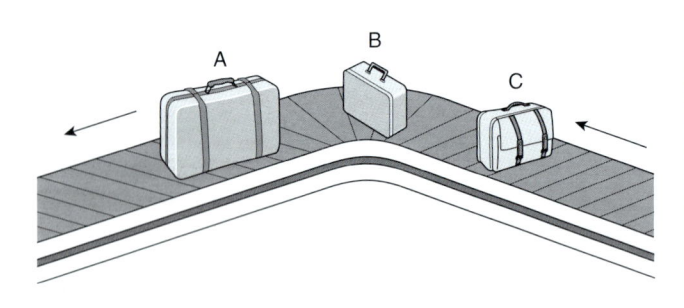

Does the momentum of the luggage change as it turns left with the conveyor belt? Give a reason for your answer. *(2 marks)*

b) Which of the following units can be used to measure momentum?
J/s   kg m/s   Nm   *(1 mark)*

6 a) The diagram shows a simple design for a space rocket.

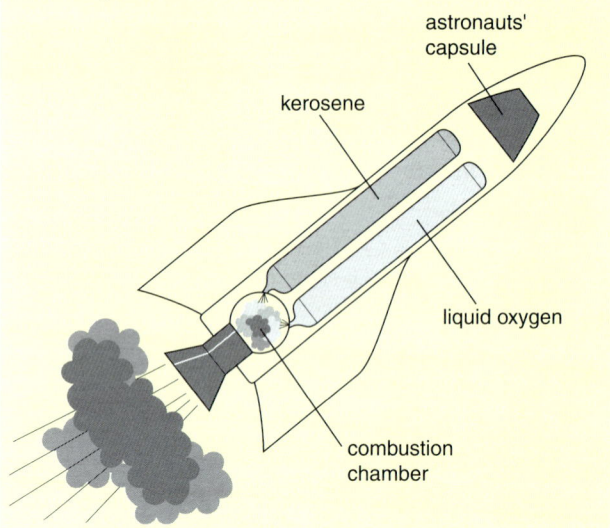

i) Explain, using the idea of momentum, how the initial propulsion of a rocket is produced. *(3 marks)*
ii) State and explain **one** way the acceleration of a rocket can be increased. *(2 marks)*
iii) In what unit is momentum measured? *(1 mark)*

b) The diagram shows an astronaut working in space. Releasing compressed gas from the back pack allows the astronaut to move around.

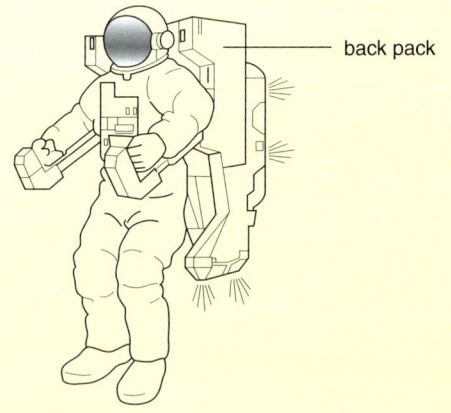

During one spacewalk, 0.5 kilograms of gas was released in 2 seconds. The gas had a speed of 60 metres per second. Use the following equation to calculate the force, in newtons, exerted on the astronaut by the gas. (Ignore the change in mass of the back pack).

$$\text{force} = \frac{\text{change in momentum}}{\text{time}}$$

(2 marks)

7 a) The picture shows two ice hockey players skating towards the puck. The players, travelling in opposite directions, collide, fall over and stop.

player 3
mass = 75 kg
speed = 4 m/s

player 4

   i) Use the following equation and the data given in the box to calculate the momentum of player number **3** before the collision. Show clearly how you work out your answer and give the unit.

      momentum = mass × velocity
(3 marks)

   ii) What is the momentum of player **4** just before the collision? *(1 mark)*

   iii) The collision between the two players is **not** *elastic*. What is meant by an *elastic* collision? *mark)*

b) The pictures show what happened when someone tried to jump from a stationary rowing boat to a jetty. Use the idea of momentum to explain why this happened.
(2 marks)

c) The diagram shows one type of padded body protector which may be worn by a horse rider.

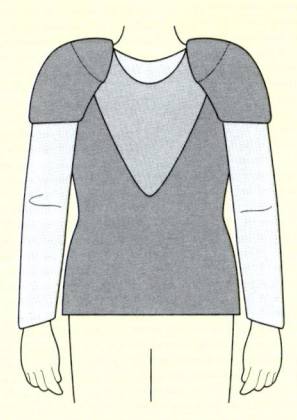

If the rider falls off the horse, the body protector reduces the chance of the rider being injured. Use the idea of momentum to explain why. *(3 marks)*

8 The diagram shows a satellite in orbit around the Earth.

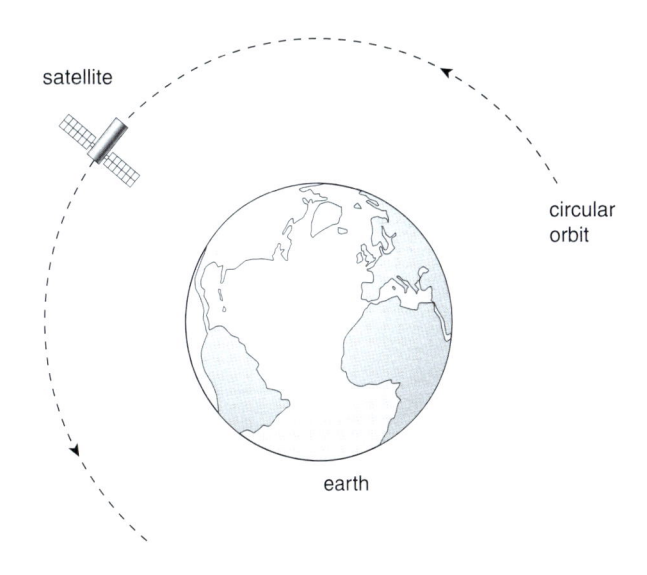

satellite

circular orbit

earth

a) Copy and complete the diagram, drawing an arrow on the diagram to show the direction of the centripetal force which acts on the satellite.
(1 mark)

b) Use words from the following list to complete the sentences.

      greater   less   unchanged

   i) If the mass of the satellite decreases then the centripetal force needed is ———— .

   ii) If the speed of the satellite increases then the centripetal force needed is ———— .

   iii) If the radius of the orbit increases then the centripetal force needed is ———— .
(3 marks)

Forces and Motion

9 The following paragraphs appeared in a newspaper.

> **JEEP FAILS GOVERNMENT TEST**
>
> A car manufacturer confirmed yesterday that one of its four-wheel drive mini-jeeps rolled over at 38 mph during stability tests conducted by the Government.
> Testing has been halted until safety cages can be fitted to seven makes of mini-jeeps which the Department of Transport has agreed to test after repeated complaints from the Consumer's Association. The Association claims its own tests show that the narrow track, short-wheelbase vehicles are prone to rolling over. The Government's tests highlight how passengers raise the centre of mass. All seven vehicles passed the test unladen, although one raised two wheels.

a) Write down **two** factors mentioned in the newspaper article which affect the stability of vehicles. *(2 marks)*

b) The diagram shows a tilted vehicle.

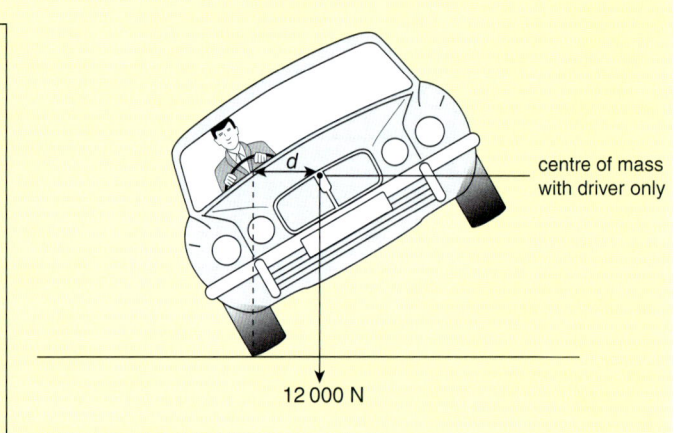

centre of mass with driver only

12 000 N

The distance **d** shown in the diagram is 50 cm. Calculate the moment of the force about the point of contact with the road. *(3 marks)*

c) Explain how passengers make the vehicles more likely to roll over (less stable). You may use diagrams if you wish. *(4 marks)*

Chapter 3
Waves

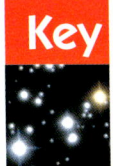

Key terms

converging lens • diverging lens • focus • real image • virtual image

3.1 Optical devices

Co-ordinated: 10.15
Modular: 14.7 mod 23

Lenses

A lens refracts (bends) light to produce an image. Many optical devices such as cameras, magnifying glasses, spectacles (glasses) and microscopes use lenses. There is even a lens in each of your eyes.

Although lenses can be made from any transparent material, they are usually made from glass. The glass lenses can be ground and polished to remove any small imperfections on their surfaces. Most, but not all, lenses have two spherical or nearly spherical surfaces.

There are two main types of lens, converging (or convex) and diverging (or concave).

Did you know?
The earliest known picture of a person wearing spectacles was painted in 1392.

Converging lenses

In general any lens that is thicker in the middle than it is at the edges is a **converging lens**.

Figure 3.1 *Converging lenses*

Light entering the lens is refracted towards the normal. Light leaving the lens is refracted away from the normal.

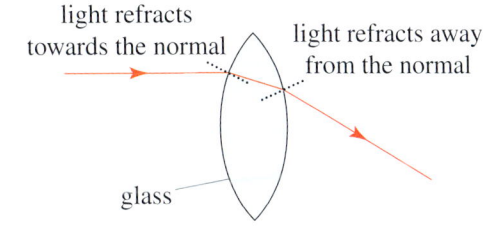

Figure 3.2 *Light refracted by a converging lens*

45

Waves

As a result of refraction, parallel rays of light entering the lens will converge to meet at a single point. This point is called the **focus** of the lens. The thicker the lens the closer the focus is to the lens.

Figure 3.3
Parallel rays of light passing through a convex lens converge at the focus

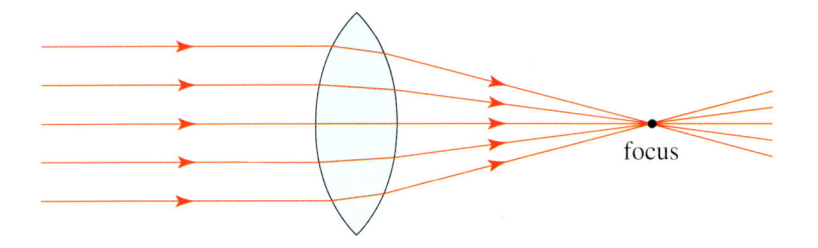

Light can pass through the lens in either direction. So parallel rays of light coming from the right would converge to a point at an equal distance to the left of the lens.

A converging lens can focus the light from a distant object onto a sheet of paper. An image of the object will be seen on the paper. The image will be sharpest when the paper is positioned at the focus of the lens.

Figure 3.4
A converging lens can be used to project an image onto a piece of paper

This sort of image is called a **real image**. When the light from an object passes through its image then it is a real image. A real image can be shown on a screen. In a camera, a converging lens is used to produce a real image of an object on photographic film. The image is smaller than the object and nearer to the lens than the object.

Figure 3.5
A camera can be used to produce a real image on photographic film

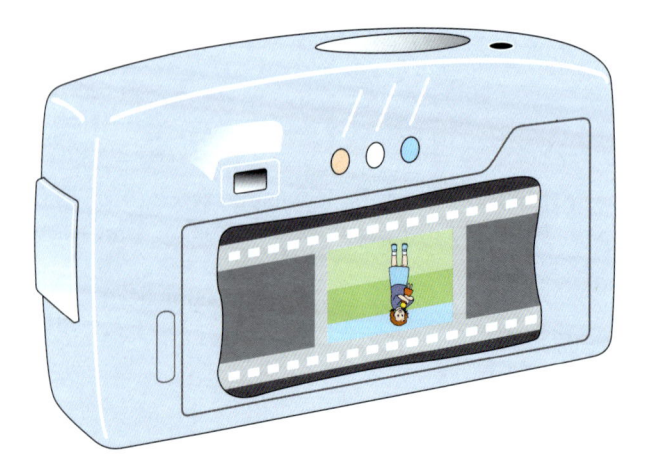

46

Optical Devices

Figure 3.6
The image produced is both smaller and nearer to the lens than the object is

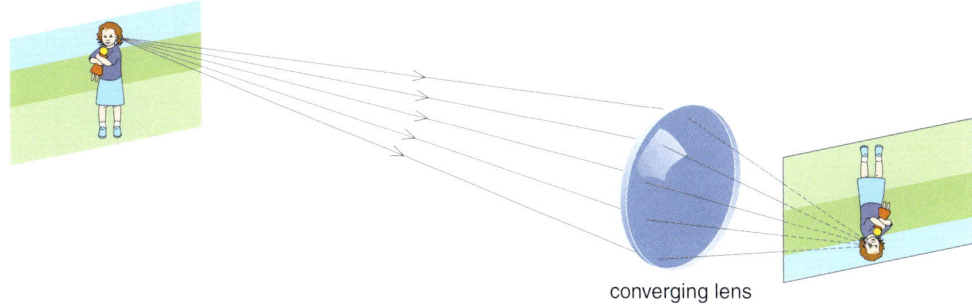

converging lens

Diverging lenses

In general any lens that is thicker at the edges than it is in the middle is a **diverging lens**.

Figure 3.7
Diverging lenses

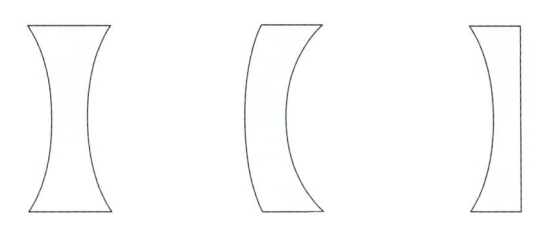

Light entering the lens is refracted towards the normal. Light leaving the lens is refracted away from the normal.

Figure 3.8
Light refracted by a diverging lens

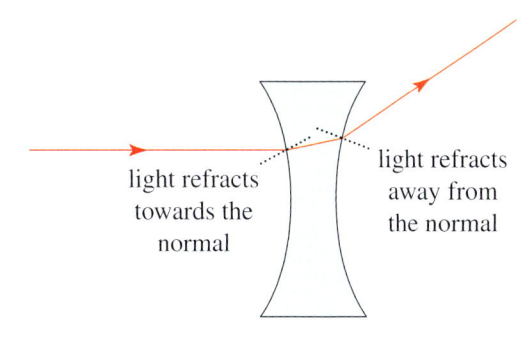

light refracts towards the normal

light refracts away from the normal

As a result of refraction, parallel rays of light entering the lens will spread out or diverge as they leave the lens. The rays do not meet at a single point but they do look as though they diverge from a single point. This point is the focus of the lens. It is a virtual focus.

Figure 3.9
The virtual focus of a diverging lens

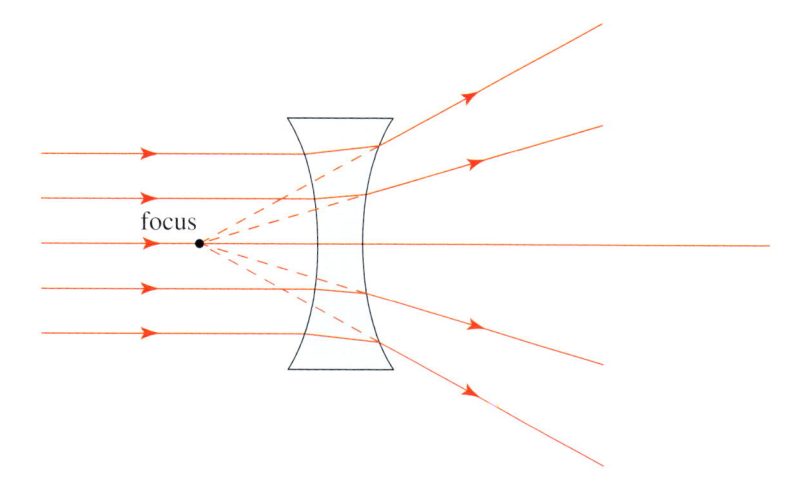

focus

47

Waves

A diverging lens always produces a **virtual image**. It is impossible to show a virtual image on a screen as the light does not actually pass through it. The only way to see the image is to look through the lens.

Ray diagrams for converging lenses

The position and nature of an image can be found by drawing a ray diagram. Two rays of light are drawn from one point on the object. Each ray of light always takes a fixed path. A real image is formed where the two rays of light cross.

It is usual to show the refraction as if it all happens at a straight line that runs through the centre of the lens. This is a simplification as refraction really happens at both surfaces of the lens.

A ray of light parallel to the axis of the lens is refracted through the focus.

Figure 3.10

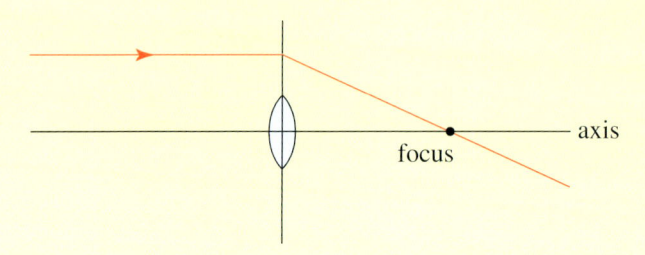

A ray of light going through the centre of the lens continues in a straight line. (Strictly this is not true, but it is a useful approximation).

Figure 3.11

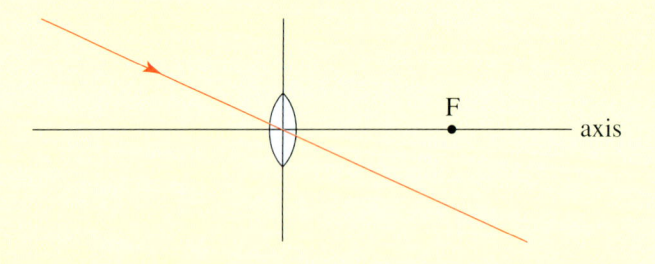

The position of the object affects the image.

Figure 3.12
The image produced for objects far from the lens

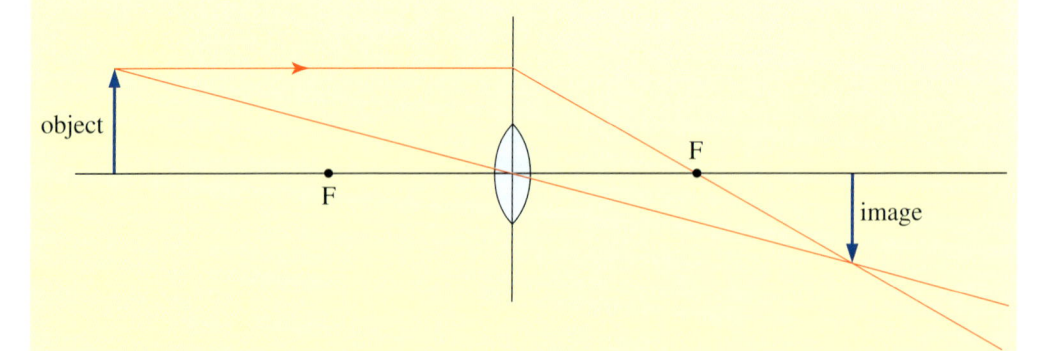

The image is:

- real,
- inverted (upside down),
- smaller than the object.

Optical Devices

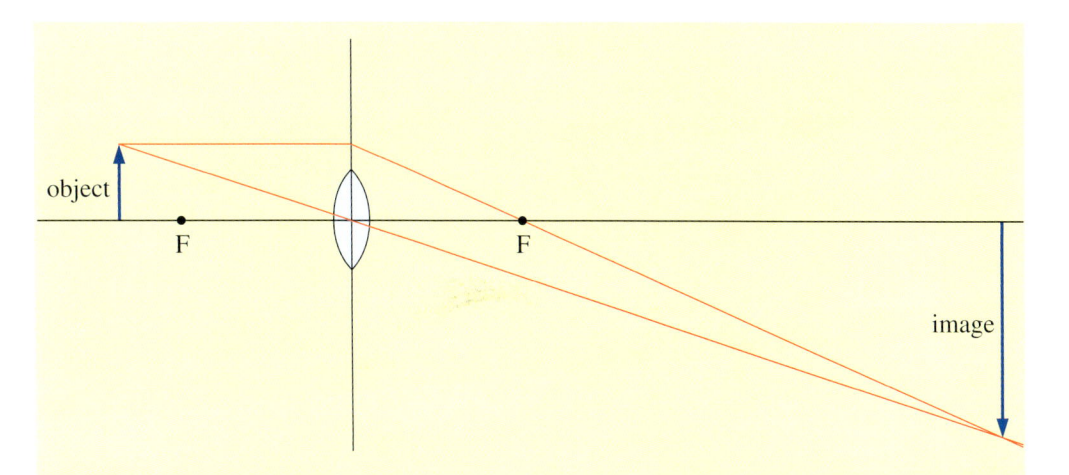

Figure 3.13
The image produced for objects close to the lens

The image is:
- real,
- inverted,
- bigger than the object (magnified).

Ray diagrams for diverging lenses

These are drawn using the same two rays of light as for a converging lens. The ray of light going through the centre of the lens will continue in a straight line. But the ray of light parallel to the axis is refracted so that it seems to have come from the virtual focus. A virtual image is formed where the two rays seem to cross.

Figure 3.14
The image produced by a diverging lens

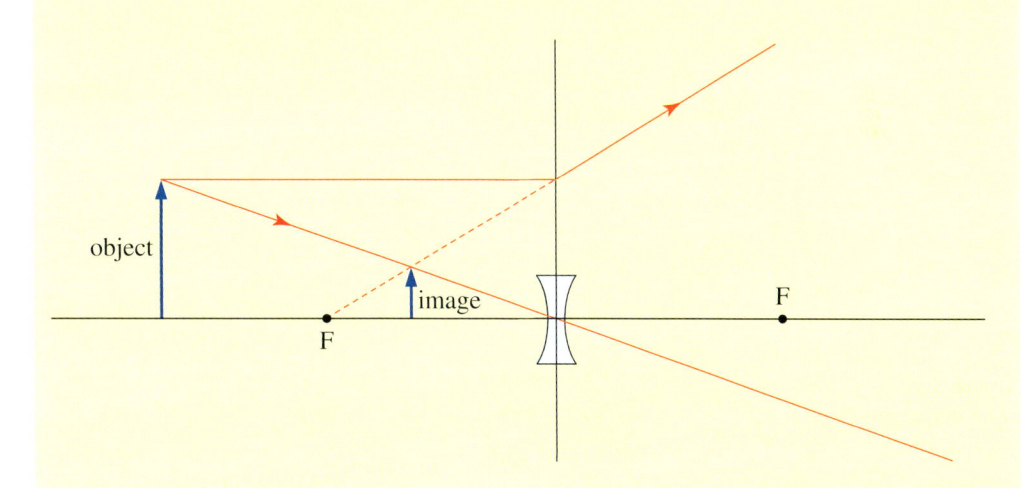

The image is:
- virtual,
- upright,
- smaller than the object.

The image produced by a diverging lens is always virtual, upright and smaller than the object.

The magnifying glass

A single converging lens can be used as a magnifying glass. The most powerful magnifying glasses use very thick lenses.

49

Figure 3.15
A converging lens produces a magnified image of a close object

Figure 3.16
When a person looks through a converging lens at a close object they see a magnified image of that object

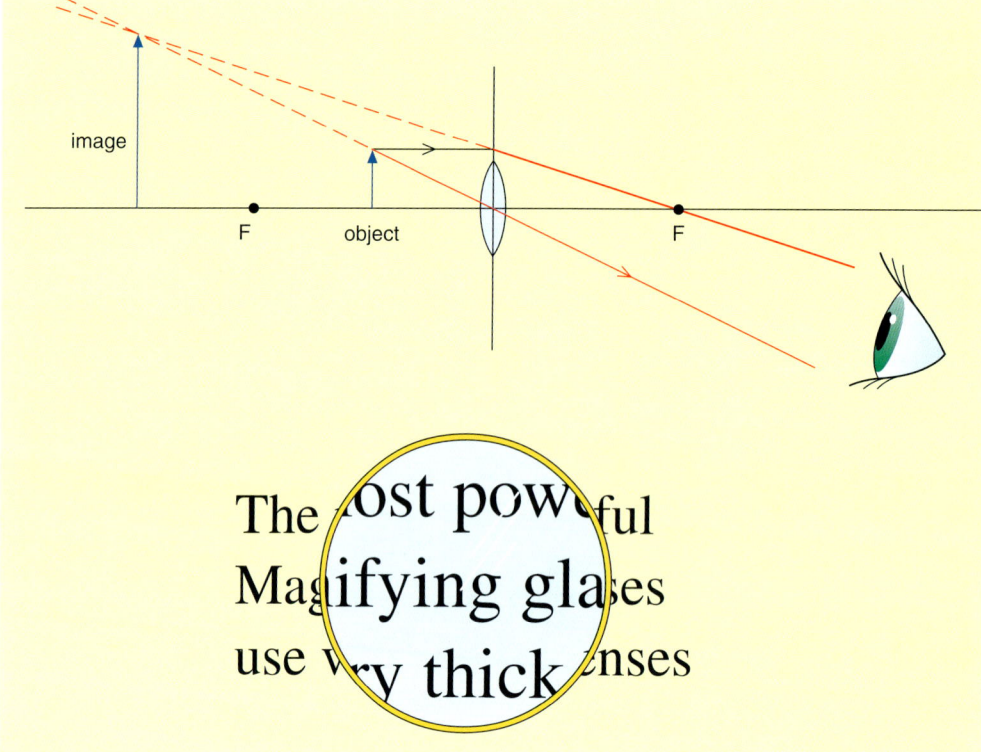

When the object is between the lens and its focus, the rays of light from the object passing through the lens do not cross over. The only way of seeing the image is to look through the lens. The image is a virtual image. It is also upright and magnified.

Did you know?

The first person to see microbes in water was Anton van Leeuwenhoek (1632–1723). He made a perfectly smooth, spherical lens from a grain of sand.

The camera

A camera uses a converging lens to produce an inverted, small, real image on photographic film.

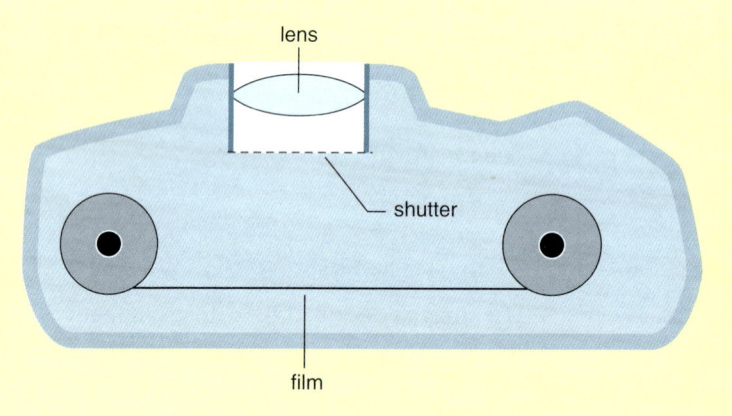

Figure 3.17
A cross section of a camera

Light reaches the film when the shutter is open. The image of a fast moving object will be blurred if the shutter is open for too long.

Optical Devices

To focus a camera the lens is moved towards or away from the film. This movement allows the camera to produce sharp images of close and distant objects. The closer the object is to the camera, the further the lens needs to be moved away from the film.

Figure 3.18
A camera lens

Summary

◆ A converging lens can produce a real or a virtual image.

◆ A diverging lens always produces a virtual image.

◆ A real image can be shown on a screen, a virtual image cannot.

◆ A camera uses a converging lens to produce a real image on photographic film.

◆ A converging lens can produce an upright, magnified, virtual image.

Topic questions

1. Copy and complete the following sentences:
    a) A _____ lens is thinner in the middle than at the _____.
    b) Parallel rays of light _____ by a convex lens will meet at the _____ .
    c) A camera produces an _____ , _____ image of an object.

2. Which of the lenses below are converging?

3 What type of image does a diverging lens always produce?

4 Describe a method to find the approximate distance between a converging lens and its focus.

5 Copy and complete each of these ray diagrams. 'F' marks the focus of the lens.

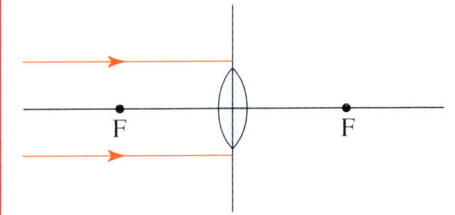

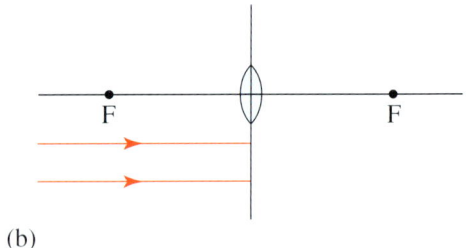

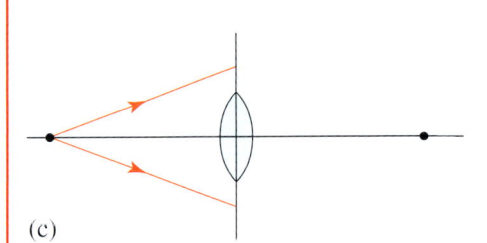

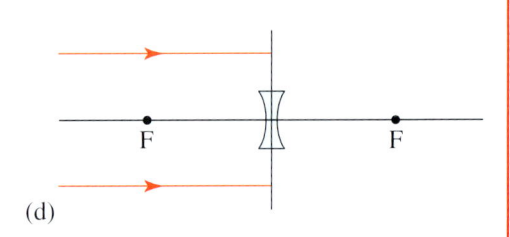

(a)

(b)

(c)

(d)

6 In a camera a lens is used to produce an image of an object on the film.
   a) What type of lens is used to produce the image in a camera?
   b) Give two ways in which the image produced on the film is different from the object.

7 Copy and complete the following ray diagram to find the position, size and type of image.

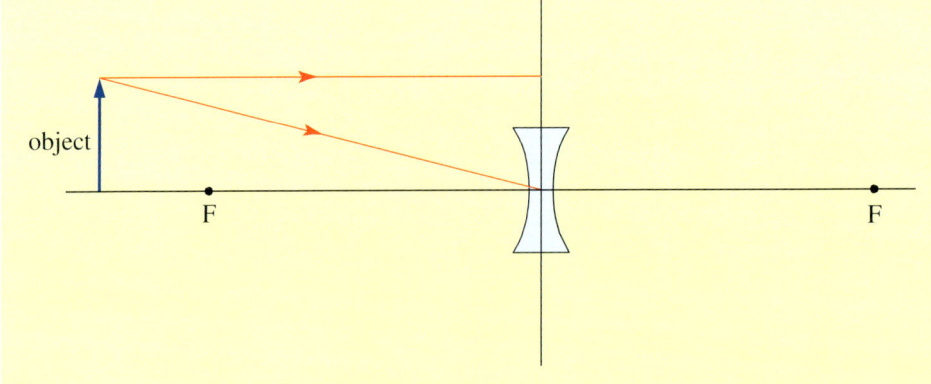

8 A converging lens is used as a magnifying glass. The distance between the centre of the lens and the focus of the lens is 5cm. An object 2cm high is placed 3cm from the lens.
   a) Draw a ray diagram to find the position, size and type of image.
   b) What magnification has the lens produced?

Examination questions

1 The diagrams below show some pieces of glass.

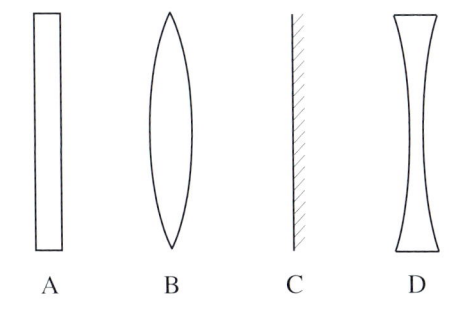

A   B   C   D

a) Which of **A**, **B**, **C** and **D** is
   i) a converging lens?
   ii) a diverging lens? *(2 marks)*
b) Copy and complete the diagram below to show what happens to the rays of light when they pass through **B**.

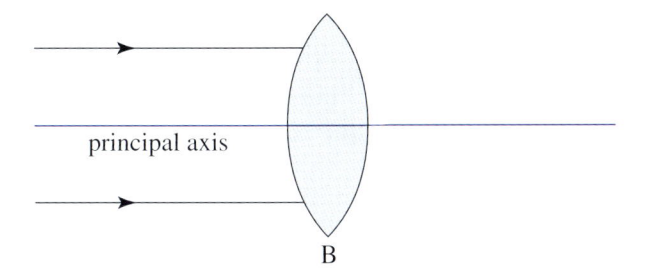

principal axis

B

(4 marks)

2 a) An object OB is placed 12 cm in front of a converging lens of focal length 9 cm. The diagram below is drawn to scale.

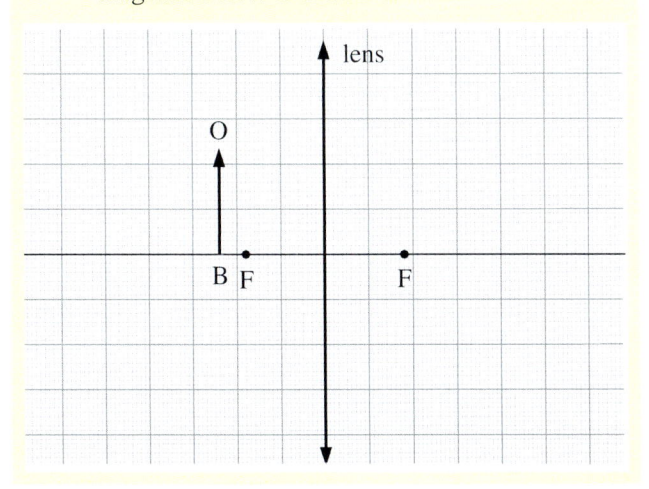

i) Draw the ray diagram on graph paper to show the position and size of the image. Draw and label the image.
ii) Write down two ways in which the image is different from the object.
(6 marks)
b) Cameras use converging lenses to produce an image of an object. Give two ways in which the image produced on the film is different from the object. *(2 marks)*

3

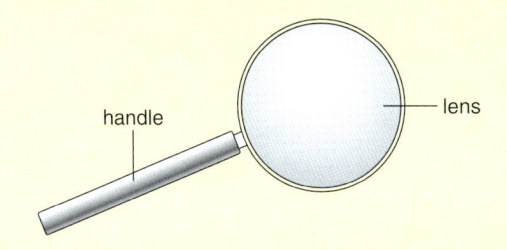

When some people are reading a book with very small print, they may use a lens like the one shown in the diagram.
a) State the type of lens used.
b) Explain, in as much detail as you can, how the lens makes it easier to read the print.
(4 marks)

53

Glossary

Capacitor A device designed to store electric charge.

Centre of mass The point where all the mass of an object can be thought to be concentrated.

Converging lens Any lens that is thicker in the middle than it is at the edges.

Diverging lens Any lens that is thicker at the edges than it is in the middle.

Elastic collision A collision that involves no overall change in kinetic energy.

Focus The point through which parallel rays of light incident on a converging lens will be refracted.

Input sensors Devices that detect changes in the environment.

Kinetic energy The energy possessed by an object due to its motion.

Logic gate A type of electronic switch used to process information.

Moment The size of the turning effect of a force, measured in Nm.

Momentum Defined as mass × velocity. Units are kg m/s.

Output device The part of an electronic system controlled by the processor. It transfers electrical energy to other forms of energy.

Pivot A point that objects turn around.

Potential divider A combination of resistors in series, used to split the voltage of a battery into two parts.

Processor The part of an electronic system that decides what action is needed.

Real image An image that can be shown on a screen.

Relay An electromagnetic switch.

Resistor A device for controlling the current in a circuit.

Transistor A device that can be used as a high speed electronic switch.

Velocity The speed of an object in a particular direction, measured in m/s.

Virtual image An image that cannot be shown on a screen.

Index

Note: Glossary entries are in bold.

A
acceleration 32
advanced electronic systems *see* electronic systems
axis of symmetry 25

B
balanced forces 27, 37
battery 11, 12
biceps muscle 23–4

C
camera 46, 50–1
    flashgun 15
capacitor 14–15, 17, **54**
car door indicator 9
centre of gravity 24
centre of mass 24–8, **54**
centripetal force 37–40
circuits 1–21
    diagram evaluation 13–14
circular motion 37–41
collision 34–5
colour coding 3
computer control 2
converging lens 45–7, 51, **54**

D
diode 14
diverging lens 47–8, 51, **54**

E
elastic collision 35, 36, **54**
electric motor 2
electronic systems 6–7, 16–17
explosion 34, 35–6

F
focus 46, 47, 48, 49, **54**
force 22–30, 34–5, 37–41
    and momentum 32–3, 36

G
greenhouse heater 10

I
image 45, 51
    in camera 50–1
    converging lens 46, 47, 48, 49
    diverging lens 48, 49
    in magnifying glass 50
input sensors 6, 12, 17, **54**
internet 17

J
joint (in body) 23–4

K
kinetic energy 31, 35, **54**

L
Leeuwenhoek, Anton van 50
lens 45–53
    concave 47–8, 51
    convex 45–7, 51
light dependent resistor (LDR) 6, 13, 14
light emitting diode (LED) 7
line of action 27, 28
logic gate 7–11, 17, **54**

M
magnifying glass 49–50
microwave oven 14
mobile phones 16
moment 22–4, 28, **54**
momentum 31–7, **54**
    and force 32–3
    and safety 33–4

O
optical devices 45–53
output device 6, 7, 17, **54**

P
pivot 22, 24, **54**
plumb-line 25, 26
potential divider 11–13, 15, 17, **54**

principle of momentum conservation 35, 36
processor 6, 7, 17, **54**

R
radio 4
ray diagram 48–9, 50
    converging lens 48–9, 50
    diverging lens 49
real image 46, **54**
refraction 47
relay 1–2, 10, **54**
resistor 2–4, 17, **54**
    see also variable resistor
robots and robotics 2, 17

S
safety devices 33–4
satellite 39
security light 9, 10
sensor 6, 12, 17
space shuttle 36
stability 27–8
switch 1, 6, 17

T
temperature control 12, 13
thermistors 6, 13
time delay device 14–16, 17
tolerance of resistors 3
transistor 1, 8, 16, **54**
truth table 7, 8, 8, 9
turning force 22–30

U
variable resistor 2, 3–4, 13, 14, 17
velocity 32, 33, 38, **54**
virtual image 48, 50, **54**

V
waves 45–53

55

Photo acknowledgements

The publishers would like to thank the following individuals, institutions and companies for permission to reproduce photographs in this book. Every effort has been made to trace ownership of copyright. The publishers would be happy to make arrangements with any copyright holder whom it has not been possible to contact:

Action Plus (26, 28 bottom, 32 bottom, 34 top, 38, 39 top); Bruce Coleman (31); Corbis (25, 32 top); Hodder & Stoughton (36); Holt Studios (10); Houghton's Horses (34 bottom); Life File (9, 14 top, 16, 33); Phillip Harris (14 bottom); Ruth Nossek (51); Science Photo Library (1, 3, 4, 7 bottom, 17, 28 top, 39 bottom, 40); Telegraph Library/Getty Images (2, 15); Wellcome Trust (7 top).

Orders: please contact Bookpoint Ltd, 130 Milton Park, Abingdon, Oxon OX14 4SB.
Telephone: (44) 01235 827720. Fax: (44) 01235 400454. Lines are open from 9.00–6.00, Monday to Saturday, with a 24 hour message answering service. You can also order through our website www.hodderheadline.co.uk

British Library Cataloguing in Publication Data
A catalogue record for this title is available from the British Library

ISBN 0 340 84780 8

First published 2002
Impression number   10 9 8 7 6 5 4 3 2
Year   2008 2007 2006 2005 2004 2003

Copyright © 2002 Steve Witney

All rights reserved. No part of this publication may be reproduced or transmitted in any form or by any means, electronic or mechanical, including photocopy, recording, or any information storage and retrieval system, without permission in writing from the publisher or under licence from the Copyright Licensing Agency Limited. Further details of such licences (for reprographic reproduction) may be obtained from the Copyright Licensing Agency Limited, of 90 Tottenham Court Road, London W1T 4LP.

Cover illustration by Sarah Jones at Debut Art
Typeset by J&L Composition Ltd, Filey, North Yorkshire.
Printed in Italy for Hodder & Stoughton Educational, a division of Hodder Headline Plc, 338 Euston Road, London NW1 3BH.